contents

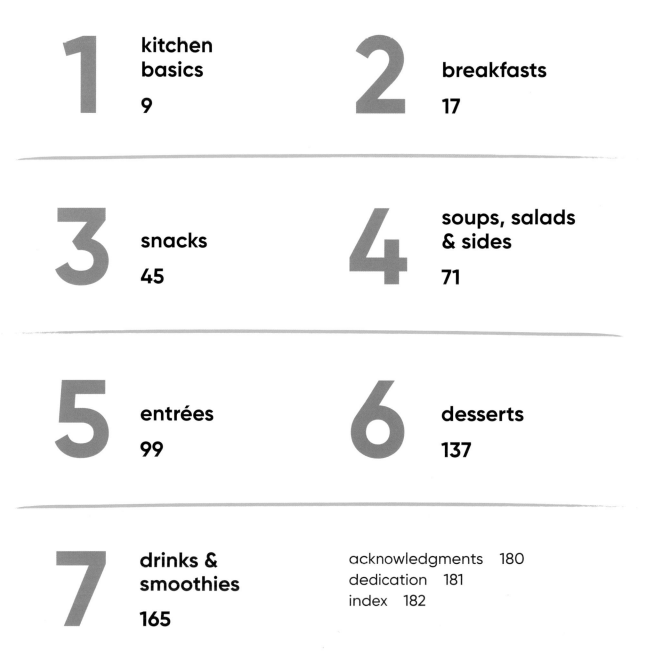

THE teen kitchen

THE teen kitchen

Recipes we
love to cook

Emily & Lyla Allen, The Kitchen Twins

Foreword by Rachael Ray

Photographs by Justin Walker

TEN SPEED PRESS
California | New York

Library of Congress Cataloging-in-Publication Data
Names: Allen, Emily, 2003- author. | Allen, Lyla, 2003- author.
   Title: The teen kitchen : recipes we love to cook / the kitchen twins,
   Emily and Lyla Allen.
   Description: First edition. | California : Ten Speed Press, 2019. | Includes
   bibliographical references and index.
   Identifiers: LCCN 2018028781 (print) | LCCN 2018032732 (ebook) |
   Subjects: LCSH: International cooking. | LCGFT: Cookbooks.
   Classification: LCC TX725.A1 (ebook) | LCC TX725.A1 A36 2019 (print) |
   DDC 641.59—dc23
   LC record available at https://lccn.loc.gov/2018028781

Trade Paperback ISBN: 978-0-399-58187-8
eBook ISBN: 978-0-399-58188-5

Printed in China

Design by Lisa Schneller Bieser
Food styling by Micah Morton
Prop styling by Paige Hicks

10 9 8 7 6 5 4 3 2 1
First Edition

foreword

Every now and then, you meet somebody with a true calling—or in the case of "the Kitchen Twins," make that two somebodies! Emily and Lyla were born to be in the kitchen. From PB&J Breakfast Bars to Sweet Pea Soup to Gingerbread Bread Pudding, their creative twists on fresh, healthy ingredients always blow me away. It brings a giant smile to my face when these young women visit my television show, and I'm excited for the world to get a double dose of delicious in their new book.

Rachael Ray

introduction

Hi! We're Emily and Lyla, and we can't wait to get cooking with you! In this book, we'll show you how to make amazing food, so you won't just have to drool over what TV chefs are making. If you're brand-new to the kitchen, we'll have you cooking like a pro in no time, and if you've been cooking for years, we have awesome tips and recipes we hope to add to your go-to lists.

In each chapter, we'll serve up a variety of recipes, from simple to sophisticated. If you're just starting out, you'll find some quick and easy recipes to get you going and then many more recipes that will take your skills and taste buds up a notch.

In addition, we'll introduce you to delicious new foods that are way better for you than frozen pizza or fast-food burgers. We're passionate about eating fresh, natural food and hope to spread the love to you!

We're excited to show you how creative, adventurous, and fun the process of cooking is. But first, we'd like to tell you a little about us—the Kitchen Twins.

how the kitchen twins got started

We started cooking when we got our first aprons and chef's hats on Christmas Day at the age of three. That day we made our first recipe, a sour cream coffee cake, with one of our grandmothers. We were so little that she had to hold us steady on chairs so we could reach the bowl and stir the batter.

We won't tell you that we instantly became master chefs, but right off the bat, we were great at licking our fingers and getting flour everywhere! We also started a tradition that day, because we still make that same coffee cake every Christmas morning with our grandmother, tweaking it along the way to make it even better (see page 159).

Around that same time, our parents started a company that made natural foods and beverages and enlisted us as taste testers. We quickly started learning to love unusual combinations like nutritional yeast and smoked paprika on popcorn, and toasted sprouted lentils paired with dark chocolate–covered cherries. (Trust us: they taste way better than they sound!)

Soon we started inventing our own recipes, and at nine, we launched our Kitchen Twins blog. A local school principal saw our blog and invited us to her school to do a cooking demo. This event made us realize how special cooking and sharing food is, because all the kids enjoyed our demo. They trusted us and that gave us confidence, especially because we were quite shy until we started talking about food and cooking.

Later that year, we won a local *Shark Tank*–style competition. We were in shock when they called our names as the first-place winners, especially because there were adults competing in the contest as well.

As our prize, we got a Soda Stream (which our dad adopted), and we were able to create a "Make Your Own Kale Chips" kit that was sold in grocery stores. Seeing our own product on a shelf was really cool; we did demos at tons of grocery stores so people could taste it, and even the so-called kale-haters were crazy about the chips.

adventures on air—hair, makeup, and of course food!

Around this time, several local TV stations, newspapers, and magazines took an interest in us. Soon, we got an invitation to compete on the Food Network's first season of *Chopped Junior*. After that, we started appearing on more shows, including *Rachael Ray* and *Today*.

It's fun to be on TV shows because we meet a lot of great people, and it inspires us to have our own cooking show someday. It's also interesting to see everything that goes into making five minutes of TV. We get a little nervous each time we do a show, but it's an excited kind of nervous. It's also cool to have our hair and makeup done by the show's stylists, and bonus: they feed us the most delicious food in the dressing room!

People often ask us how we get ready for a TV appearance. Before we do a cooking demo, we practice each recipe over and over again, and we work on who is going to say what (although this doesn't always work out—more on this later). We also have techniques we practice before we go on air to help us relax and get our mouths moving, like playing a warm-up game called "zip, zap, zop" or repeating "Unique New York" a bunch of times. So we don't just wing it. We prepare, so we feel confident before we go on stage—although we still make mistakes, like the time we sent flour flying everywhere on the *Rachael Ray* set or when we accidently licked our fingers while the camera was on us.

Once we get on the stage, our nerves go away and it's fun. We tend to disagree over whose turn it is to talk, so we pinch each other on the thigh to say, "Okay, it's my turn now." You won't see this on camera—but now you'll know why one of us occasionally winces!

We realize we have an advantage because we have each other for support in case one of us forgets to say something, messes up, or needs some boosting. *Chopped Junior* was definitely more stressful than most shows because it was a competition, and we were also competing against each other (while rooting each other on). But it was an awesome experience, and we had fun tricking the host, Ted Allen, when we switched tables and hair accessories and pretended to be each other. It worked, he was totally thrown off, and we think he was suspicious about who was who after that.

We've learned that a thirty-minute show can often take a full day of filming. For instance, it's hard to redo a food shot if we mess up while we're pouring an ingredient into a bowl, because we can't take that ingredient back out. Also, the camera operator likes to take different videos of what we're doing from different angles. And we might have to do lines over and over again because one of us flubs it.

We've been very lucky to meet celebrity chefs, including Rachael Ray, Marcus Samuelsson, Daphne Oz, Laila Ali, Daniel Boulud, Chloe Coscarelli, and Tia Mowry. We absolutely adore Rachael Ray—she's very supportive of us, enjoys showing people how fun and easy cooking is, and is a huge animal lover like us. Tia Mowry came to our home to film a FoodNework.com feature and to one of our grocery store demos, where we became three total goofs, blowing up latex gloves into balloons and probably scaring off all the customers. And Chloe Coscarelli, who's also a huge animal lover, a really great vegan chef, and wonderful mentor, kindly delivered our thirteenth birthday cupcakes to us—best present and cupcakes *ever*.

about being twins

We were born at 11:57 p.m. and 11:59 p.m. at a hospital in New York City. Our mom was freaking out, because she wanted to make sure the doctor didn't give us two different birth dates.

Before we were born, the doctor told our parents that one of us was a boy, so our parents picked out the names Katy and Matt. Then, when they found out we both were girls, our mom wanted to give us really original first names—something unique like her first name, Cricket—while our dad wanted something more traditional. They wound up picking Emily and Lyla; coincidentally, the "ly" at the beginning of Lyla is also at the end of Emily.

We're inseparable best friends and happen to have a lot in common—friends, hobbies, and yes, we look alike. Do we get sick of each other and fight? Oh, yes. We're told we are like an old married couple: one minute we're nagging and bossing each other around, and the next minute we're shoulder-to-shoulder watching TV.

Having a twin gives you a built-in best friend—there's always someone to hang out and play cards with, throw lacrosse balls to, steal clothes from, and cook with. Our parents laugh at us because if one of us goes out without the other, we call each other right away and ask, "What are you doing?" Either we miss each other or—more honestly—we just want to know if one of us is having more fun than the other or getting some sort of treat the other is missing out on.

We get asked all the time if we are competitive. YES! We keep tabs on things to make sure we're equal, such as who fed the cats last, emptied the dishwasher, sat in the front seat, got to shower first, or ate the last raspberry. (This exhausts our parents.) And we most definitely like to win A.T. E.V.E.R.Y.T.H.I.N.G!

Of course, as you can imagine since you are reading our cook-book, our number one favorite activity is cooking—together, alone, as a family, with friends, whenever, wherever. As twins, we think it's kind of cool to see how we each approach an ingredient when we're creating a recipe. It's fun for us to take a single ingredient and create different dishes, with neither of us knowing what the other is doing.

Take peas, as an example. We did a blog post and *Rachael Ray* episode called "Two Peas in a Pod." The whole point of it was to show how one ingredient can go in many directions, with one of us creating a Sweet Pea Soup (page 80) and the other a Sugar Snap Pea Sauce. So yes, we're a lot alike, but while we are indeed two peas in a pod, we do have different qualities and personalities . . . and even different scars. (We'd tell you how many, but then you might think we're klutzy.)

People often ask us whether we have different food preferences. Sometimes our tastes match, but sometimes not. We're both wild about Asian cuisines, but Lyla is fond of black olives and Emily isn't. Lyla's favorite flavor of Ben & Jerry's ice cream is Chunky Monkey, while Emily's is Cherry Garcia (and neither one likes the other's favorite). Lyla loves espresso, while Emily is so-so about it. Neither likes pulp in OJ. Lyla could put cilantro on anything and everything, but Emily prefers Italian parsley. And overall, we'd say that right now (it could change in a week), Lyla has more of a savory tooth and Emily more of a sweet tooth. So even though we're twins, we have minds of our own when it comes to food.

Now that you know a little about us, we invite you to join us in the kitchen, to share in our favorite recipes and the hobby we most enjoy. In the next chapter, we'll start out by sharing some tricks that help us out—and after that, we'll serve up dozens and dozens of our favorite recipes, along with more stories about our adventures in and out of the kitchen. Get ready to explore the process and enjoy the food!

1
kitchen basics

We love trying new foods and cooking techniques. As a result, we get pretty adventurous in the kitchen. However, when you're just beginning to cook and experiment, it's a smart idea to start out simple. You'll see that some of our recipes are super-easy, such as Frambled Eggs (page 22) and Parmesan-Crusted Grilled Cheese (page 109), and others are more complex. (That's one of the great things about cooking: There's endless stuff to cook!) Even if you're a brand-new chef, you'll find something that's easy to make and delicious to eat.

Once you get comfortable in the kitchen, you'll discover that it's fun making entrées and appetizers for groups or for special occasions. Some of our favorite foods to share with friends and family include Tomatillo Guacamole (page 56), Pumpkin Wonton Raviolis (page 103), and Smoky Deviled Eggs (page 49). Another great special occasion dish is Zucchini and Squash Galette (page 116), which is easy and delicious and looks pretty impressive. People trust us now to make the holiday dinner or appetizers for a party, but it took a little time.

For now, put on some music, find some recipes that look like fun, and enjoy the rhythms, sounds, and aromas of your sizzling kitchen. You'll have a ball, and you'll probably end up kicking everyone out of the kitchen and making it your own domain.

To help you get started, we'll share some basics in this chapter, including handy kitchen vocabulary and tips for using and substituting ingredients. In addition, we'll say a word about mistakes. The bottom line: They happen, and always will. The key, as we'll explain, is to turn them into a learning experience (or even find creative ways to turn mistakes into new and better recipes).

Before we start, however, we want to talk about the most important thing in the kitchen: safety. You may eyeroll, but taking it seriously earned us more freedom and trust in the kitchen. Some of these tips may seem obvious, but at one point we didn't know this stuff so we're erring on the side of safety.

our top safety rules

When you're cooking, you want to have fun and enjoy eating what you made, and to do that, you need to avoid getting burned, injured, or sick. Here are our top tips for preventing kitchen catastrophes.

First, don't wear long or droopy sleeves. These can catch on fire if they get too close to a burner, or get caught on things on the counter or a pan handle. We always wear short sleeves or roll up our sleeves. (You'll also avoid stains on your sleeves this way.)

The same goes for long hair. We tie ours back or put it in a ponytail. That way, it doesn't get too close to a burner or wind up in the food.

If you're new to slicing with knives, start with a small paring knife—or even a butter knife, if you're very young. As you get more skilled, you can move on to bigger knives.

When you're cutting with a knife, curl your fingers inward. This way, if you cut yourself, you won't slice a finger badly; instead, you'll merely scrape your knuckles. (See photo, page 57.)

Pay close attention to what you're doing—especially if you're cooking a dish over high heat or cutting up veggies with a sharp knife. If you look away, something might catch on fire or you might cut yourself. We say this because kitchen time is often social time as well, so it's easy to get distracted.

When you take something hot out of the oven, use two good pot holders or oven mitts. Dish towels are too thin, and you can get a bad burn. Our favorite pot holders are silicone, because nothing slips and they're completely heatproof (plus they double as a hot plate).

Always keep pan handles turned in toward the middle or back of the stove. This is especially important if you have little brothers or sisters who might try to grab them.

To keep your cutting board from slipping, put a kitchen towel underneath it.

If you have a gas stove and the pilot light (the flame below the burner) goes out, turn off the stove right away. The pilot light can be relit, but we ask a parent to do this.

Clean up spills quickly so no one slips on them. Also, if you use a nonstick spray, be careful not to let the spray get on the floor. It's slippery, and you don't want to take a nosedive. (Experienced here.)

Practice good kitchen hygiene. Wash your hands after handling raw meat, seafood, or eggs because they can contain dangerous germs, and wash cutting boards or other surfaces touched by these foods because you don't want to contaminate other foods you're preparing. (This may already be obvious to you, but anytime we do a cooking demo, we talk about this—and even on *Chopped Junior* and in other chefs' kitchens, we hear the same instructions.) Also, rinse fruits and veggies before you use them to remove germs or pesticides. This even includes lemons, limes, and oranges. Put leftover food away quickly, rather than letting it sit on the counter for hours, because food left at room temperature can breed some nasty germs.

By the way, we all know everyone drops food on the floor. If you're our mom, you throw it away. If you're our dad, well, you know. Our grandmother (GrandMolly) just watched Lyla do some beautifully decorated toast toppings, and then plop went the toast, face down on the floor. Lyla picked it up to eat it and GrandMolly said, "No way, throw it away." Generally, if you can't wash it off, trash it.

Finally, make sure you turn things off. We always double-check the stove and oven when we're done. We learned this through experience because sometimes we'll be fifteen minutes out in the car and we need to turn around because our mom can't remember if she turned something off. Yes—another eyeroll—we're sure you can relate.

good-to-know cooking terms

Now we want to introduce you to another aspect of cooking: the "language" of chefs.

We picked up lots of these terms just by hanging out with our parents in the kitchen—for instance, they showed us the difference between caramelizing an onion and just sautéing it until it's transparent, and taught us when to mince, dice, or chop—but if you're new to the kitchen, you might be new to kitchen vocabulary as well. To help out, here's a quick glossary.

Baking: Cooking food dry in the oven, covered or uncovered.

Boiling: Cooking food in water that's rocking and rolling, with big bubbles on the surface.

Broiling: Cooking food using the oven broiler (ovens have broilers in different parts—top or bottom). This involves really intense heat that will brown food very quickly, or burn it if you aren't careful.

Caramelizing: Cooking a food until the sugar in it browns. You can caramelize sugar itself or caramelize foods that contain sugar, such as onions.

Chiffonading: Slicing a leafy food (typically basil) by stacking the leaves and then rolling them up lengthwise and thinly slicing the roll or cutting it with scissors. (We sometimes just cheat and use a pizza cutter to chiffonade rather than a knife.

It's really easy to get nice strips, and it does a good job of bruising the basil so the oils come out.) By the way, *chiffonade*, a French word, is pronounced "Shif-Oh-Nod."

Chopping: Cutting food into pieces—about ½ to ¾ inch long.

Creaming: Beating sugar and softened, room-temperature butter together until they're light and fluffy.

Dicing: Cutting food into small pieces—about ¼ inch long (or about the size of your pinky fingernail).

Finely Chopping: Cutting food into very small pieces—about ⅛ inch long (or about half the size of your pinky fingernail).

Mincing: Cutting food into very tiny pieces. For the most part, you'll be doing this with garlic.

Roasting: Cooking food at a high temperature in the oven, resulting in browning or crisping of the food.

Sautéing: Cooking food quickly in a skillet in a little oil or butter over medium-high heat.

Simmering: Cooking a liquid so that it's hot enough to form tiny bubbles but not hot enough to boil.

Finally, here's another term you've heard if you watch cooking shows—*mis en place*, which means "everything in place" in French. It means making sure you have every ingredient and every kitchen tool you'll need before you start, and prepping ingredients up front (for instance, chopping onions or measuring out spices). *Mis en place* makes cooking a lot easier, and it also saves you from discovering halfway through a recipe that your sister used up the last of the bananas.

EXPERIMENT!

Be open to trying new ingredients. If you don't like a new food the first time, give it another chance. It's just like hearing a new song; sometimes, if you keep listening to it, you start liking it more and more.

Here's a good trick: If a food doesn't win you over the first time you taste it, try it a different way the second time. For instance, Emily doesn't like roasted fennel, but she enjoys topping baked potatoes or toast with fennel seed and Parmesan butter (a simple combo she did for Rachael Ray). She would have missed out on this favorite topping if she'd given up on fennel after her first try.

a word about mistakes

The chefs on cooking shows make even the most complicated dishes look easy, but that's because they've been cooking forever and they often have the *mis en place* done beforehand (plus, they can film another take if they mess up). In the real world, you're bound to make mistakes, whether you're a pro or a beginner.

If you mess up while cooking, don't get (too) upset. It's a learning experience and makes you better. For example, Emily was making cupcakes once and put in too much apple cider vinegar while experimenting with a vegan version. They were disgusting, and they found the garbage quickly. As a result, she'll be avoiding vinegar cupcakes from now on. Another time, we made a lasagna and didn't cover the top layer of noodles with sauce, just a sprinkle of Parmesan. The result was a hard, cardboardlike top layer of lasagna we had to pull off and throw away. (We ate the bottom part, though—we were hungry!) That's another mistake we won't make again.

Sometimes, you can roll with a mistake and reinvent a dish. For instance, chef Cesar, whom we interviewed in New York—a chef who works with one of the top chefs in the world, Daniel Boulud—burned some rice he was making. He scraped off the rice and the scrapings ended up a little like chips, giving him the idea to make some amazing and unique rice chips. So his mistake turned into a successful recipe that never would have happened without the goof.

Another time, Lyla was making thin mints and had just coated them in chocolate when the whole tray dropped onto the floor (face up) and cracked. That gave her an idea, and now she cracks the cookies instead of cutting them into small bites in our recipe for cookie brittle on page 150.

fun food swaps and our commonly used ingredients

Before we head for the recipes, we want to talk a little bit about some of our favorite ingredients— and about what to do if you don't have them on hand.

First, if you're missing an ingredient, don't panic. It's usually easy to find a substitute. You'll find basic substitution charts online, and here are some of our personal favorites as well.

Don't have rice? Use quinoa or couscous. You can substitute any one of these three grains for another; just follow the directions on the package.

Don't have eggs, or avoiding eggs in your baking? Try chia "eggs" or aquafaba.

- Chia "eggs": To replace 1 egg, mix 1 tablespoon chia seeds with 3 tablespoons water, stir, and let sit for 5 minutes. The mixture will thicken to an egglike consistency. We often use this in place of eggs when we're baking.

- Aquafaba: This is the liquid in a can of chickpeas. It is thick and similar in consistency to a whipped egg. The general rule we follow is to use 2 tablespoons of aquafaba to replace 1 egg. If your mixture looks really dry, add in another tablespoon of aquafaba.

Substitute onions for shallots. Note that onions will take longer to caramelize.

No sweet onions? Use regular white onions. (We like the sweet onions because of the taste, and they seem to make us cry less.)

Substitute plain full-fat yogurt for sour cream or mayonnaise. (We prefer Greek yogurt because of the texture and tart taste.)

Short on softened butter to spread on grilled cheese? Use mayonnaise instead.

Don't like tofu? Use chicken. (Or vice versa.) It's pretty easy to swap out something vegetarian for a meat, or the other way around.

Don't have coconut oil? Softened butter or a neutral-flavored oil will work, too.

Next, here are some helpful tips about ingredients we frequently use in our recipes:

When a recipe calls for milk, you can use any type of dairy milk (nonfat, low-fat, or whole) or substitute nut, coconut, or soy milk, unless a recipe specifically calls for a certain type of milk. There are two types of coconut milk—the type in the large carton, and the canned type. When our recipe calls for canned full-fat coconut milk, do not swap this for the coconut milk in a carton or for low-fat canned coconut milk. It is definitely not the same.

When a recipe calls for salt, we like to use pink Himalayan salt (fine or from a grinder) because it contains valuable minerals and it's not bleached like regular table salt. However, sea salt will do just as well. You can also use regular table salt if that's what you have on hand.

When a recipe calls for applesauce, we like to use smooth, unsweetened applesauce (and when we can, we make it ourselves—page 26).

If a recipe calls for maple syrup, don't substitute pancake syrup. Trust us: You want the real thing.

If a recipe calls for pepper, use freshly ground pepper if you can. If you can't, just add a few pinches of preground black pepper.

If a recipe calls for oat flour, you can buy it or make your own from rolled oats (see Twin Tip on page 142).

If you don't want to commit to buying a whole bag of an ingredient like nuts or chia or hemp seeds, you can always just buy a little bit for a recipe from the bulk bins in grocery stores.

Finally, be sure to check our notes and tips in the recipes! The notes at the end of each recipe will help you master that specific recipe, and the tips will increase your overall cooking skills and kitchen know-how.

2
breakfasts

In spring and early summer, our calendar is filled with lacrosse tournaments. This means waking up early and loading up all our to-go breakfast foods, such as PB&J bars (page 23) and Cinnamon Banana Overnight Oats (page 30)—anything that travels well.

On weekends with no tournaments, we sleep in. Then we immediately gravitate toward the kitchen, for three reasons: We love to eat food, we want to make food, and we're hungry. We immediately manage to make a mess—because, as you can imagine, we don't just pour ourselves a bowl of cereal!

First, we make a small breakfast, like a smoothie (see chapter 7) or Avocado Toast (page 20), and photograph it for a post. (We take turns doing this job.) Now we're hungry, so we have to eat our pretty food shot. And yeah, we may have left a mess . . . so we slyly leave the kitchen and do our homework on the couch. (This bugs our parents, because they keep setting up new desk areas that we ignore.)

Of course, all that homework makes us hungry . . . and this leads to another, bigger breakfast and a second photo shoot, leaving our kitchen in even more dish distress. Sometimes we'll leave the mess just long enough for us to get in trouble—or magically, someone will clean it up. Our kitchen is ALWAYS messy, but in a well-loved sort of way.

Whether it's a busy weekday or a late-waking weekend at your house, this chapter will help you out with good and filling breakfast options. We offer a variety of recipes for all palates and cooking levels—sweet, savory, simple, complicated, make-ahead, and on-the-go eats. So we hope to have you full and happy after this most important meal, or meals, of the day!

avocado toast

MAKES 1 SERVING   PREP TIME: 5 minutes

1 large slice sourdough
bread

½ avocado

1 tablespoon sliced almonds

½ teaspoon extra-virgin
olive oil (see Twin Tips)

Salt and freshly ground
black pepper

twin tips

If possible, use a high-quality
olive oil, especially when you
are using it raw (for instance,
on toast or in salad dressings)
or as a coating. Good olive oil
is darker and more "greenish"
than lower-quality oil.

Do you ever wind up with stale
bread, end pieces of bread,
or pizza crust? We save these
and make them into croutons.
We just dice them up, toss and
coat them with olive oil, throw
them in a greased sauté pan
with a sprinkle of fresh or dried
herbs, and sauté them until
they're browned and crunchy.

Avocado toast is one of our favorite things to enjoy for breakfast,
or for a quick dinner after a late after-school event. Quick, easy,
healthy, tasty = done! This may not seem like "cooking," but you're
making it at home—so we say it counts.

Lightly toast the bread. Scoop out the avocado half onto a cutting
board and mash it with the back of a fork.

Spread the mashed avocado on the bread, sprinkle with almonds,
and drizzle with olive oil. Add salt and pepper to taste and serve.

frambled eggs

1 teaspoon unsalted butter

2 eggs

Toasted, buttered bread
(optional)

Salt and freshly ground
black pepper

What are frambled eggs? They're eggs that are half scrambled,
half fried, and totally delicious.

Frambled eggs are an easy solution when you just can't decide
what type of egg you want, or you try to make a fried egg and it
breaks when you flip it (a common story in our household).

A special thank-you to Aunt Kimmy, who introduced this mistake-
free egg recipe to us. We added the brown butter because
it tastes so good, and coined the word *frambled*. This is our
favorite type of egg, and we hope it's soon to be yours.

Heat a nonstick skillet over medium-low heat and add the butter.

Let the butter get bubbly and caramel-colored, gently stirring as it
does. This will take about 1 minute.

When the butter is ready, crack the eggs one at a time and gently
slip them into the pan.

Cook until the whites are set, about 1 minute, then flip each egg.

Once you've flipped the eggs, immediately break the yolks with the
sharp end of the spatula and then gently break up the whites and
scramble the whites and yolks together until they are the desired
consistency. This will take about 30 seconds to 1 minute.

Put the eggs on top of a buttered piece of toast, season with salt
and pepper, and enjoy.

pb&j breakfast bars

MAKES ABOUT 18 BARS   PREP TIME: 10 minutes   COOK TIME: 25 minutes

2 cups old-fashioned rolled oats

A couple pinches of salt (we use pink Himalayan sea salt)

1 teaspoon ground cinnamon

3 tablespoons chia seeds (optional)

1 cup smooth, unsweetened applesauce (see Notes), store-bought or homemade (page 26)

⅔ cup peanut butter (creamy or crunchy)

¾ cup of your favorite jam (we prefer raspberry or strawberry)

We call these breakfast bars, but that's only because we like to grab them on our way out the door in the morning. In truth, we reach for these bars all day long. They have a ton of protein and fiber from the peanut butter and oats, so they keep us full during long days at school. Are they healthy? Yes, but they're also soooooo good. Even Rachael Ray is a huge fan!

If you don't have any chia seeds on hand, don't worry—it won't change the taste. They boost the nutrition, but these bars are super-healthy even without them.

Preheat the oven to 350°F. Line a 9 by 13-inch baking pan with parchment paper.

In a medium bowl, mix the oats, salt, cinnamon, and chia seeds. Add the applesauce and peanut butter and mix well so the ingredients are evenly distributed.

Spoon the mix onto the parchment and press down evenly with your hands to make a uniform layer. On top, spread your jam all around so it covers the entire surface. Bake for 25 minutes.

Wait for the bars to cool, then cut into rectangles. Store in an airtight container in the fridge for up to 5 days (if they last that long).

NOTES

Chunky applesauce is good, but it doesn't work in these because the result is a dry bar. So stick with smooth.

You can make these into sandwiches by cutting two even-size bars and putting the jam sides together sandwich style. This is a great way to pack the bars for travel because they stay neater.

carrot cake pancakes

MAKES 12 TO 20 PANCAKES (depending on size)

PREP TIME: 12 to 15 minutes   COOK TIME: 20 to 25 minutes

2 eggs

½ cup milk

½ cup smooth, unsweetened applesauce, store-bought or homemade (recipe follows)

1 tablespoon vegetable oil

1¼ cups unbleached all-purpose flour, whole-wheat flour, or oat flour (see Twin Tips page 142)

2 teaspoons baking powder

2 teaspoons ground cinnamon

¼ teaspoon salt

¼ cup packed light brown sugar

2 cups peeled, shredded carrots (about 2½ carrots)

Butter or applesauce with a drizzle of maple syrup or honey, for topping (optional)

We enjoy these pancakes for breakfast and then pack up a few in a to-go container because they make a delicious snack.

We prefer to shred the carrots by hand or use the shredder blade on a food processor rather than buying preshredded carrots at the store for this recipe, because the preshredded carrots are too thick and long (they are matchstick-size rather than shredded).

We use unsweetened applesauce for this recipe, but you can use whatever you have—or you can make your own applesauce using the recipe on page 26.

In a large bowl, whisk the eggs and then add in the milk, applesauce, and oil.

In a medium bowl, mix the flour, baking powder, cinnamon, salt, and sugar. Mix the dry ingredients into the wet ingredients. Then add the carrots and mix until they're well blended.

Heat a nonstick griddle over medium heat. (A drop of water should sizzle on it.) When it's ready, add a little butter or cooking spray to the surface.

Add 1 to 2 tablespoons of batter for each pancake. Cook for about 3 minutes per side, until golden brown. You can test for readiness by pushing the spatula down on the pancakes. If no batter oozes out, they are done and ready to eat. The first few pancakes always seem to take a touch longer, so be patient! Top with butter and syrup and serve. If you have leftover cooked pancakes, store them in an airtight container in the freezer for up to a month and pop them in the toaster or the oven to reheat and enjoy.

applesauce

MAKES 4 CUPS (8 half-cup servings)
PREP TIME: 15 minutes   COOK TIME: 20 to 25 minutes

5 large apples (we usually use Fuji apples)

½ cup apple juice

twin tip

If you have bruised apples, don't throw them away—use them to make applesauce.

Yes, you can buy applesauce—but homemade is so much better, and incredibly easy! We eat it straight all the time and also enjoy it with pancakes, yogurt, oatmeal, and baked potatoes. You'll see applesauce in many of our recipes because it's so versatile.

Core the apples and chop them into 1-inch cubes. (You don't need to peel them.) Be sure to use as much of the apple as possible.

Add the apples and apple juice to a large saucepan. Cover and cook over medium-low heat for 20 to 25 minutes, stirring occasionally, until the apples are soft.

Remove from heat and let the apples cool for 5 minutes. Add the apples and their juice to a blender and blend to the desired consistency; serve warm or chilled. This will keep in the refrigerator for 5 days and in the freezer for a month.

granny's pancakes

1 egg

1 cup milk

1 tablespoon sugar

1 tablespoon vegetable oil

1 scant cup unbleached all-purpose flour (*scant* means just under a cup; see Twin Tips)

2 teaspoons baking powder

Cinnamon sugar or maple syrup for topping

twin tips

Never pack down flour when you're measuring it. Instead, spoon the flour lightly into your measuring cup and level it off with the straight side of a knife. If a recipe calls for a scant cup, just take a small spoonful from the top so it's not level.

When you measure flour, always use a dry measuring cup—the kind that doesn't have a pour spout—because then it's easier to level it off.

Our mom is not really a pancake person, because she doesn't like what she calls "dense cakes of fried flour." However, she was a big fan of the pancakes her Granny used to make. They were super-light, and they were the only traditional-style pancakes our mom would eat.

Here is her Granny's recipe for super-light pancakes, taken from our mom's pencil-scribbled notes as a child. We think her Granny would be psyched.

In a medium bowl, whisk together the egg, milk, sugar, and oil. In a small bowl, mix the flour and baking powder. Add the dry mixture to the wet.

Heat a griddle over medium heat. (When it's ready, a drop of water should sizzle on it.) Add a little butter to the surface, and let it melt and disperse.

Ladle the batter onto the griddle (about 2 tablespoons per pancake). Wait until the pancake bubbles, then flip. Regrease the pan when needed.

Enjoy with a sprinkling of cinnamon sugar or maple syrup. Keep any extras in the freezer; they will keep for up to a month. To reheat, pop them in a toaster.

maple granola

1 cup old-fashioned
rolled oats

½ cup sliced almonds

½ cup unsweetened
shredded coconut

½ cup unsalted shelled
sunflower seeds

½ cup chopped pecans

2 tablespoons melted
coconut oil

3 tablespoons maple syrup

⅛ teaspoon salt

twin tip

Nuts get rancid fast at room
temperature—so if you buy
nuts in bulk, store them in the
freezer. That way, they'll stay
fresh for a year.

One reason we got into cooking is that we like our homemade
stuff way better than store-bought. That's not bragging; it's just
that fresh tastes better. When you make a recipe by hand, it
shows in the result.

For instance, you can buy a million brands of granola at the
grocery store, or get cute versions at specialty stores that cost
like $10 a bag—but nothing will taste quite as good as your own.
Here's a really simple granola recipe that you can change up if
you like (maybe switch up the nuts and seeds, or add some dried
fruit) to put your own stamp on it.

This granola is tasty all by itself, but here are some other great
ways to use it: add it to an Açai Bowl (page 40); top your favorite
ice cream with it; make a parfait by repeating layers of yogurt,
granola, and fruit in a pretty glass or to-go jar; or top a bowl of
sliced bananas with granola, put a little nut butter on top, and
microwave until the nut butter is all melty.

Preheat the oven to 325°F and line a baking sheet with parchment
paper.

Mix the oats, almonds, coconut, sunflower seeds, and pecans
together in a large bowl. Then mix in the oil, maple syrup, and salt.
Make sure it's all combined well, and spread the mixture on the
parchment.

Bake for about 20 minutes, flip and stir the granola, and bake for
5 to 7 more minutes. The granola should be a nice golden/bronzed
color. Remove from the oven and let cool on the pan. Serve or store
in an airtight container for a week at room temperature, or a month
in the fridge.

cinnamon banana overnight oats

MAKES 1 SERVING   PREP TIME: 5 minutes

¼ cup old-fashioned rolled oats (not quick oats)

1 tablespoon unsweetened shredded coconut

1 tablespoon sliced almonds

⅛ teaspoon ground cinnamon

Pinch of salt

¼ cup plus 1 tablespoon milk

½ teaspoon packed light brown sugar (you can taste-test and add more in the morning if you wish, but the banana also sweetens this)

½ banana, thinly sliced

twin tips

Here are two additional ways that jars come in handy:

Peeling hard-boiled eggs. Fill a jar halfway with water and add a hard-boiled egg. Shake hard, and the eggshell will come off.

Peeling garlic. Add your garlic cloves to a jar and cover. Shake hard, and the "paper" on the outside of the garlic will come off.

We're big into "jar food"—that is, food we can create and serve in a jar that we've recycled—because jars make for a perfect to-go meal. Generally, 14- to 15-ounce jars are perfect. Covered glass or plastic containers work fine, too.

This recipe is simple because there's no cooking involved. You just dump the ingredients into a jar, give the jar a good stir or shake, let it sit in the fridge overnight, and your breakfast is ready to go in the morning. By then, the oats have absorbed the flavors of all the goodies, so it's really delicious.

This is a great "power food" breakfast, especially good for endurance days that involve tests, sports, or binge-watching *Gilmore Girls*! If you've had muesli before, this will remind you of it.

Put the oats, coconut, almonds, cinnamon, salt, milk, brown sugar, and banana in a jar. Mix until well combined and put in the fridge overnight. Enjoy at home or on your way anywhere.

VARIATION

Switch out the nuts and fruit for whatever your favorites are. We like to use walnuts and diced strawberries, or pecans and diced apple.

grilled pb&j sandwich

MAKES 1 SERVING   PREP TIME: 5 minutes   COOK TIME: 5 minutes

1 tablespoon unsalted butter, softened

2 slices bread (any type)

1 tablespoon peanut butter (creamy or crunchy)

1 tablespoon of your favorite jam

This is a toasty twist on regular PB&J. Peanut butter really fills us up, so this is awesome breakfast fuel, and it's easy to prep and cook before you run out the door. Pressing the sandwich with a lid gives the bread a good crunch, elevating this beyond the standard PB&J.

Spread the butter on one side of each slice of bread. Spread the peanut butter and jam on the non-buttered sides of the bread. Put the two slices together with the peanut butter and jam on the inside.

Grease a medium skillet and place over medium heat. Add the sandwich to the pan and put a flat metal lid on top to lightly press down the sandwich. After 1 minute, using a pot holder to lift the lid, check and see if the sandwich is golden brown and toasty on the bottom. When it is, flip and cook until it's golden brown and toasty on the other side. This will take 1 to 3 minutes per side.

Cut into quarters and enjoy.

a day in the life of our food

Weekday mornings at our house are controlled chaos—burners sizzling, the Vitamix humming, jars clanking, knives chopping, the fridge opening and closing, and our big photography lights coming in and out so we can take pictures of our food. All four of us at once are tossing stuff together to eat right there, such as Frambled Eggs (page 22), or to take out the door, like Grilled PB&J Sandwiches (page 31).

If we have time, we'll be civilized and eat breakfast sitting down—but that's only because our dad will ask us if we think we're at Stanley's lunch counter (basically, that's his hint to sit and eat, not stand).

We leave for school around 7:20 with a load of books, food, and sports equipment. The twin who took the morning's food photo does the social media posts on the way to school (and does the evening posts, too). We take turns sitting in the front seat; we had to work this out because even though we're each other's best friend, we argue about stuff like that.

For lunch, we love to have leftovers or things that we can quickly whip up in the morning. For example, we'll bring Golden Black Beans (page 128), Cheesy Rice Cakes (page 126), or Mediterranean Stuffed Peppers (page 129). A couple of years ago, we'd take a photo of our lunch every day on weekdays and post it. Now we don't do that because it takes up too much time in an already busy enough day!

After school when we have sports we don't get home until after 6:00. Our family always tries to have dinner together, missing only an occasional night. We enjoy having some sort of dinner ritual as well; for instance, we'll share a new word or read a passage from the book *How to Eat* (you should check it out). In our house, the person who makes dinner gets the good end of the deal. That's because we love cooking, and our rule is that the person who makes dinner doesn't have to clean up.

At night, we do homework and chores, such as taking care of our cats, Sapphire and Pearl. We'll then try to read for a while if we're not too tired. This is usually where our hectic day ends and the next begins!

33

open-faced quesadilla with fried egg

MAKES 1 QUESADILLA   PREP TIME: 5 minutes   COOK TIME: 5 minutes

One 6-inch flour or corn tortilla

⅓ cup shredded sharp Cheddar cheese

⅓ cup black beans, drained and rinsed

¼ teaspoon smoked paprika

1 tomato, thinly sliced

½ avocado, thinly sliced

1 egg

Salt and freshly ground black pepper

twin tip

If you spot Kumato tomatoes at the store, try them, because they're full of flavor. Beware, however, they're an ugly brown-ish purple, so don't judge them by their looks. Any tomatoes will work, but these are our favorite from the grocery store (although we prefer the tomatoes we get from farm stands in the summer—they are the best).

Fried egg yolks are kind of like gravy—so we thought, why not put an egg atop a cheesy quesadilla and have it ooze out like gravy when we cut into it? We keep this quesadilla open-faced so we can taste more of the ingredients, not just the tortilla.

Place a skillet on the stove over medium-low heat and lightly coat it with cooking spray or olive oil. Add the tortilla to the pan and sprinkle the cheese on top of the entire tortilla.

Spoon the beans on top of the cheese. Sprinkle the smoked paprika over the cheese and beans and let everything sit for about 1 minute so the cheese starts to melt. Once the tortilla is crispy and lightly browned on the bottom, move it to a plate and top it with the tomato and avocado.

Keeping your skillet on the heat, add a bit more oil and crack the egg into the skillet. When the white starts to harden and turn opaque, gently flip the egg. It will need to cook for about 1 minute per side. If the yolk pops, don't worry; you can just "framble" the egg (see page 22).

Place the fried egg on top of the quesadilla, season with salt and pepper, and serve.

popeyes

1–2 tablespoons mayonnaise or softened unsalted butter (enough to slather on both sides of the bread)

1 slice bread

1 egg

Salt and freshly ground black pepper

Why do we call this recipe Popeyes? Because our grandfather did, so our mom did, and so we do now. Other names people have shared with us include eggs-in-a-basket, egg-in-a-hole, birds-in-a-nest, toad-in-a-hole, hens-in-a-basket, Egyptian eye, dropped eggs on toast, circle eggs, and finally, cowboy eggs. How fun is it that one simple dish has so many names? They're probably passed down from generation to generation, just like in our family.

There's a good chance you've had these before, but we have some tips for making them even better.

Spread the mayonnaise or softened butter on each side of the bread. Make sure you spread it over every single centimeter of your bread, because you don't want to cheat yourself out of grilling perfection!

Using a 1-inch biscuit cutter or the mouth of a small glass, cut a hole in the center of the bread.

Place a skillet over medium heat and add cooking spray or a dab of butter to grease the surface. When the skillet is hot, add the bread and the circle you cut from it. Toast both pieces on one side, and then flip.

When the bread is golden on both sides, crack the egg into the center hole. When the white starts to turn opaque, gently flip to cook on the other side. Cook until all of the white is opaque and not jiggly. (Be careful not to burn the little circle. You can remove it before your egg is done.) Sprinkle with salt and pepper to taste.

NOTES

We like to add more circles by spreading butter or mayo on another piece of bread and making circles from the whole thing. One circle is never quite enough!

Don't use margarine or low-fat mayo. They're soft, but definitely not as good as butter or full-fat mayo in our opinion. Mayo is super-easy to spread, so it's probably our preferred choice here.

We grill the bread on both sides a bit before we add the egg because we don't want to have to flip this more than once and risk breaking the yolk. We are picky about this.

anytime waffles

4 tablespoons unsalted butter

3 eggs

1 tablespoon sugar

1¾ cups milk

1½ cups unbleached
all-purpose flour

1 tablespoon baking powder

¼ teaspoon salt

Toppings (optional, see below)

While waffles are mostly a breakfast food, we enjoy them just as much for lunch or dinner with savory toppings—either open-faced or as a regular sandwich. We offer a variety of options below for savory or sweet waffles.

By the way, as we were developing this recipe, we decided that *waffle* is just the weirdest word. Say it over and over again, and you'll see what we mean.

Preheat the oven to 200°F. Melt the butter and let it cool a bit.

In a medium bowl, beat the eggs, sugar, and milk.

In a separate bowl, mix the flour, baking powder, and salt. Add the mixture to the wet batter and mix in the melted butter.

Grease a waffle iron. When it is hot, ladle ¼ to ⅓ cup of batter into each waffle area. Close and cook for about 4 minutes each. Using a fork or tongs, carefully transfer the cooked waffles to a baking sheet and place in the warm oven until you're ready to serve them. Add a topping from the options below and serve.

If you have leftovers, you can freeze your extra waffles. Just put them in a zip-top plastic bag after they have cooled down. They will keep in the freezer for up to a month. Pop them in the toaster or oven to reheat them.

TOPPING OPTIONS

SAVORY

Top with avocado, egg, bacon, soy Fakin' Bacon (see Notes, page 123), and/or cheese.

Top with caramelized onions and cheese.

Use two waffles as "bread" to make a BLT (bacon, lettuce, and tomato sandwich) or grilled cheese sandwich.

SWEET

Top with maple syrup, jam, butter and cinnamon sugar, or honey and yogurt.

Top with ice cream and chocolate sauce or caramel sauce, or with grilled fruit.

Top with nut butter, sliced bananas, slivered almonds, and chopped pecans.

açaí bowl

One 3.5-ounce packet of
pure, unsweetened, frozen
açaí berry

¼ cup milk

¼ cup strawberries or
blueberries (fresh or frozen)

1 ripe banana

Sliced bananas, Maple
Granola (page 29), and /
or sliced strawberries for
topping

Açaí bowls are kind of like a slowed-down smoothie. They're a little thicker, and we serve them in a bowl so we can eat them in a more thoughtful and polite way. We say this because normally we chug down smoothies, and our parents ask if we even tasted what we just swallowed. (Sound familiar?)

Anyhow, açaí bowls are good and very photo-worthy, especially if you get artistic with your toppings. But beware if you're wearing white clothes, because açaí stains.

Add the açaí berry, milk, strawberries, and banana to a blender.

Blend until smooth, spoon into a bowl, and add the toppings of your choice.

omelet with caramelized onions and cheese

MAKES 1 OMELET PREP TIME: 10 minutes COOK TIME: 5 minutes

1 tablespoon extra-virgin olive oil

¼ sweet onion, diced

3 eggs, beaten

1 tablespoon water

3 tablespoons shredded sharp Cheddar cheese

twin tips

Crack your eggs on the inside of a bowl or glass measuring cup, so that no egg oozes down the side. This tip comes from our mother, who gets annoyed when there's raw egg on the counter.

If you get shell in your bowl, use a metal spoon or the eggshell itself to scoop up the shell. Both seem to attract the shell pieces.

A while ago, we received a set of fancy nonstick pans from an Italian cookware company after we did a little work with them. As a result, we discovered that omelets are awesome!

While we're putting this recipe in the breakfast category, we often make it for dinner, paired with a salad and French fries drizzled with truffle oil. (This is a great way to use up any truffle oil you have left over from making our Cauliflower Truffle Lasagna, page 131.)

Add the olive oil to a small or medium nonstick sauté pan and sauté the onion over medium heat for 5 to 10 minutes, or until transparent with golden, caramelized edges.

Meanwhile, whisk the eggs in a small bowl and add the water. Remove the onion from the pan, leaving the heat on.

Add the eggs to the pan, and don't touch! Let them cook for about 2½ minutes, until the omelet looks almost solid and isn't jiggly. Spoon the sautéed onion and cheese onto half the omelet. Carefully flip the other half of the omelet over the half with the filling, so it looks like a half-moon. Cook for about 1 more minute, until all of the eggs are set and cooked through.

NOTES

If you are cooking more than one omelet, sauté 1 whole onion and do your omelets in stages. When we make these for dinner for our family, we plate them on ovenproof plates and put them in the oven on low (200°F) to stay warm.

The time it takes to caramelize the onions will depend on your pan size and the volume of onions in your pan.

sweet crumb-topped blueberry muffins

MAKES 12 MUFFINS   PREP TIME: 15 minutes   COOK TIME: 20 to 25 minutes

MUFFINS

2 eggs

1 teaspoon vanilla extract

½ cup plus 3 tablespoons unsweetened, smooth applesauce, store-bought or homemade (page 26)

¼ cup vegetable oil

½ cup plus 1 tablespoon sugar

1½ cups unbleached all-purpose flour or gluten-free flour

1 teaspoon ground cinnamon

1 teaspoon baking powder

½ teaspoon baking soda

⅛ teaspoon salt

1 overflowing cup blueberries (fresh or frozen)

TOPPING

3 tablespoons sugar

1 teaspoon ground cinnamon

½ cup old-fashioned rolled oats (not quick oats)

2 tablespoons cold coconut oil or unsalted cold butter, diced

We hate it when a muffin has a good topping but skimps on the rest, like it doesn't count. These, however, are good from top to bottom. They have a sweet textured topping and a good dose of blueberries, so every bite from the first to the last is delicious.

We owe our mother a big debt for providing the ingredients for many batches of this recipe, and for serving as our taste-tester. Baking is a science, and when we set out to write this cookbook, the baking recipes required far more testing than anything else. (That's because one little variation can change the whole outcome.) Luckily, our mother went along with our quest for perfection—a goal we think we've achieved here.

Preheat the oven to 350°F and grease a 12-count muffin pan (or use liners).

To make the muffins, in a large bowl, whisk together the eggs, vanilla, applesauce, and vegetable oil. In a separate medium bowl, mix the sugar, flour, cinnamon, baking powder, baking soda, and salt. Add the dry ingredients to the wet ingredient bowl and mix. Add the blueberries and stir well.

Using a cookie scooper, equally distribute the batter among the muffin cups.

To make the topping, in the emptied dry ingredient bowl, stir together the sugar, cinnamon, and oats, then add the coconut oil. Using your fingers, mash the coconut oil together with the dry ingredients so the coconut oil is in little bits about the size of a pencil eraser and has the dry ingredients clinging to it.

Sprinkle about 2 teaspoons of the topping on each muffin and then, using a fork, prick the topping into the muffins, gently pressing down so the oats cling to the top. Bake for 20 to 25 minutes. At the 20-minute mark, insert a knife; if it comes out clean, the muffins are done.

Store in an airtight container for 2 to 3 days. We usually keep these goodies in the fridge rather than on the counter, because they stay fresher that way.

twin tips

We use a silicone muffin pan. It works much better than a metal pan, because the muffins pop out easily. We're pretty sure our pan was a gift, and it's a good present to put on your own wish list.

If you use a metal muffin pan, we recommend using liners. This makes it easier to get the muffins out and clean the pan.

3
snacks

We were thinking about how many snacks we have during the day, and we realized that it's about a dozen—mixed nuts, bars, deviled eggs, dip and veggies, edamame, yogurt, fruit, more bars. Our mom coaches at our school, and people probably think we're spoiled because when she arrives, she's always delivering more homemade snacks. What can we say? We are hungry people.

We're also big on fresh, natural ingredients. If you look in our fridge and pantry, you'll see that we don't have many processed foods. (Our two exceptions are blue tortilla chips and a huge box of Honey Nut Cheerios.)

Do we sometimes buy snacks from the store? Sure, but we like the homemade stuff best. When we buy a snack, we rarely finish it because it's just not as good. Plus, we swear we get canker sores if we eat a lot of packaged foods.

Snacks are a fun way to get inventive, and you can create the exact type of snack you're craving. Here's a sampling of our favorite snack-time creations to suit any mood. You can eat them any time, or occasionally do what we do: skip a traditional meal and go for what we call a "happy meal" created entirely from snacks.

smoky deviled eggs

MAKES 12 DEVILED EGGS   PREP TIME: 20 minutes   COOK TIME: 15 minutes

6 eggs

¼ cup plain full-fat Greek yogurt

¼ cup mayonnaise

2 teaspoons ketchup

1 teaspoon smoked paprika, plus more for serving

½ teaspoon cumin

⅛ teaspoon salt

¼ teaspoon sriracha hot sauce (optional)

twin tip

Don't peel hard-boiled eggs just before having guests over, because your house will stink. The same goes for cooking broccoli or cauliflower.

Smoked paprika is the key ingredient here. It has to be the smoked version, not regular paprika, because non-smoked paprika doesn't have much flavor.

These eggs have been a longtime signature recipe of Lyla's, because she adopted smoked paprika very early and discovered that it added great flavor to a deviled egg.

Sriracha is something we've really developed a taste for, because our dad is a spice freak. Our mom, not so much—but she does enjoy it in these eggs, because it's more a flavor enhancer than a light-your-mouth-on-fire kind of spice.

One interesting thing we discovered when we had friends and family test this recipe is that there are lots of different ways people boil their eggs. Our approach works great, but feel free to use your own.

These are a favorite snack of ours, and also great to serve at a party or during the holidays.

Fill a saucepan halfway with water. Add the eggs, making sure the water covers them by an inch. Bring the water to a boil, then reduce the heat to a simmer and cook the eggs for 8 minutes.

When the eggs are done, pour the hot water out of the pan. Refill the pan with cold sink water and add a couple of big handfuls of ice cubes to cool the eggs.

To peel the eggs, crack them and roll them gently on paper towels to create more cracks. Peel off the shells, rinsing and drying each egg after you've peeled it. (Alternative: Try our technique for peeling eggs in a jar, see page 30.)

Slice the eggs in half. Using a small spoon, scoop out the yolks and put them in a bowl. Mash the yolks with the back of a fork. Add the yogurt, mayo, ketchup, smoked paprika, cumin, salt, and sriracha. Mix well, until smooth and creamy. Then use one of these methods to stuff your deviled eggs:

Use a little spoon to add a dollop of yolk filling to each white.

Pipe the filling into the whites. To do this, put an opened plastic zip-top bag in a cereal-size bowl and roll the sides of the bag outside the bowl. Scoop all of the filling into the bag. Snip ⅛ inch off one corner of the bag, so you can pipe the filling through the hole to fill the egg whites.

Once the eggs are filled, sprinkle each one with smoked paprika. Store the finished eggs in the refrigerator for up to 2 days.

smothered popcorn

MAKES 4 SERVINGS   COOK TIME: 10 minutes

2 tablespoons vegetable oil

⅓ cup popcorn kernels

⅔ cup peanut butter

¼ cup plus 1 tablespoon honey

There are many ways we enjoy popcorn—savory, spicy, and sweet—but this version is definitely a crowd favorite. A national magazine featured this recipe when we were twelve because they thought it would be very POPular, and we hope you agree.

By the way, we eat this with a spoon. You'll see why.

Put the oil and the kernels in a large pot with a lid. Turn the heat to high until you hear the popcorn kernels start to pop. Then turn the heat to medium and shake the pot lightly every few seconds until no more kernels pop.

When the kernels are done popping, turn the heat to low. Remove the lid, add the peanut butter and honey, and mix until the ingredients are melted and "smother" the popcorn. Serve this in individual bowls with spoons.

NOTE

Popcorn cooks very differently on an electric stove compared to a gas stove, and we find that it can burn more easily on the electric. Just be mindful and turn the heat down a bit if it smells like it's burning.

share the food, share the fun, and share your stories with us!

What's even more fun than cooking? Sharing your cooking and food adventures. Here are some ways to connect, cook, and eat with your friends:

Host a themed potluck or start a foodie club.

Plan a potluck or put together a monthly foodie club with a group of friends based on a special theme—brunch, dim sum, dessert, ethnic food, finger foods, breakfast for dinner, vegetarian, or whatever you all like. The only rule: Everything has to be homemade. You can even pick a specific cookbook (like this one!) and everyone brings a dish made from that book.

In fifth grade, we had a big vegetarian potluck and yoga party. We had a yoga instructor come with her fifteen-year-old daughter, who'd just received her certification. We all made vegetarian dishes and shared them after we did yoga.

Our mom has a foodie club that meets once a month. She and her friends get together at someone's house, and they each bring a dish with a common theme. Everyone gets to try dishes they've never tasted before, and then they all share their recipes. It's kind of like a book club for foodies.

Have a food crawl.

In a food crawl, you go to a variety of places to taste different foods. Here's how we did it. For our birthday, we invited friends to go on a walking and tasting tour around town. This was prearranged with the stores and restaurants so we had a map telling us where to go. We went to six different places:

A spice shop, where we tasted crazy-spicy ghost peppers and then a variety of different spices on cucumbers.

Olive oil specialists, where they gave us samples of olive oils from around the world and told us what gave each one its unique color and taste.

A cheese shop, where we tasted goat, cow, and sheep's milk cheeses and had to guess which was which.

A chocolate shop, where they had American and European chocolates for us to try.

An awesome crepe café—where we all shared quarters of the cinnamon, sugar, and butter crepes.

A cupcake shop, where we ended the crawl with birthday cupcakes, of course.

Host your own *Chopped* party.

First choose a recipe category, such as breakfast, appetizer, or dessert. Then have a "judge" pick out four ingredients you need to use in the dish. If you're cooking in teams, give each team its own basket. One ingredient in each basket should be offbeat, while the other three should be more familiar. Aim for challenging, but not impossible. (Here's one to try—flour, eggs, pickles, and potato chips.) Also, make sure you have plenty of basics on hand (spices, oil, onions, garlic, and so on), enough utensils for everyone, and enough space for multiple cooks.

You and your friends can compete as individuals or as teams. Unveil the baskets, set the timer for thirty minutes, and have a judge pick the winners, or simply enjoy the fun of cooking and see if you create something tasty (or at least funny). When the two of us do this on our own, we pick out each other's ingredients and judge each other's results.

When we were preparing to go on *Chopped Junior*, we'd have our friends or family give us a basket. They'd time us and taste the dishes at the end. Long after we went on the show, we still love to take this challenge. It is fun and it gives us even more confidence to be creative in the kitchen.

Connect with our community.

Join us on social media, where you can make new foodie friends, find inspiration, and share your stories. Follow us on Instagram, Twitter, Snapchat, Facebook, and YouTube; visit us at our blog, kitchen-twins.com; and post your own food pics with #theteenkitchen. We can't wait to see what you're up to in the kitchen!

INSTRAGRAM: kitchentwins
TWITTER: kitchentwins
FACEBOOK: /kitchentwins
SNAPCHAT: kitchentwins
YOUTUBE: Kitchen Twins

sesame edamame

5 cups (or 18 ounces)
frozen edamame in the pod

1 teaspoon toasted sesame oil

¼ teaspoon salt

1 teaspoon sesame seeds

This is a lot like eating buttered popcorn, because you'll keep licking your fingers in between pods of edamame. If you don't feel like doing that, keep a napkin nearby—but don't take too many pauses to clean up, because these will be gone in a flash.

This is a snack we have often because edamame pods have a ton of protein, vitamin C, and calcium—who knew?

Cook the edamame according to package directions, but without salt in the water. Do not overcook.

When the edamame pods are done, strain and rinse them under cold water, put them in a bowl, and dry them well with a towel. Drizzle on the sesame oil and toss. Sprinkle on the salt and sesame seeds and toss well.

To eat edamame, put a pod in your mouth, slide the beans out of the pod with your teeth, and toss the pod. (We put out a separate bowl for the discarded pods.) Messy but fun.

beautiful beet dip

MAKES 6 SERVINGS   PREP TIME: 10 minutes

1½ cups plain Greek yogurt (2% or full-fat)

¼ cup extra-virgin olive oil

1 tablespoon plus
1½ teaspoons honey

2½ teaspoons white wine vinegar

¼ teaspoon salt

1½ cups precooked chopped beets (about 3 large beets, or 8.6 ounces; see Note)

Tortilla chips, veggies, fresh slices of red or green cabbage, apple slices, or wonton chips for dipping

twin tip

Measure your olive oil in the measuring spoons first, then reuse them for the honey. This way, the honey will slip right out.

This dip is a very cool color of purple. It doesn't look natural, but it is. It has a little sweetness to it, so we like to pair it with salty tortilla chips for a sweet-and-salty combo.

You may say, "Eh, I don't like beets"—but our friend's younger brother, who literally would not eat a veggie if you paid him, loved this dip and single-handedly finished the bowl. (He actually stuck his fingers in the bowl so he could own it.)

Add the yogurt, olive oil, honey, vinegar, salt, and beets to a food processor and blend until smooth and creamy. Serve with tortilla chips.

VEGAN VARIATION

The vegan version of this dip is just as dynamite and it's an easy adjustment; just follow the recipe, but make these changes: Increase the amount of olive oil to ½ cup. Replace the yogurt with ½ cup firm plain tofu. Replace the honey with just under 2 tablespoons maple syrup.

NOTE

You can buy precooked beets in the produce section of most stores. We prefer the Gefen and Love Beets (plain) brands. Or you can also make this dip with fresh beets you roast yourself. Here's how to do it. Preheat the oven to 400°F. Wash whole beets, dry them, and peel them. (To keep the mess to a minimum, wear kitchen gloves and an apron, peel the beets into a bowl in the sink, and then slice them into chunks.) Coat the beets with a little olive oil. Wrap all the beets together in a piece of aluminum foil, place them on a baking sheet, and roast them for 45 minutes. Remove the foil and let them cool before chopping them up.

tomatillo guacamole

MAKES 4 SERVINGS   PREP TIME: 10 minutes

4 tomatillos

½ peeled avocado

10 cherry tomatoes,
2 Campari tomatoes, or
1 large tomato, sliced

2 tablespoons chopped
sweet onion

¼ garlic clove (about
⅛ teaspoon minced)

2 tablespoons extra-virgin
olive oil

1 teaspoon red wine vinegar

¼ teaspoon salt

Tortilla chips for serving

twin tip

An avocado is ripe if it's turning dark and "gives" a little when you press on the skin. If it's bright green and hard, it's unripe. If it's squishy, it's overripe. There's nothing worse (in our house) than opening a brown avocado. Luckily, there's an easy way to avoid this problem. If you buy a bunch of avocados and they all start to get ripe at the same time, just stick them in the fridge and they'll stop ripening.

We were first introduced to tomatillos at our school, because they grow in the school garden. They're kind of weird looking, because they have a green paperlike shell on them (which is their husk). When you peel them, they look like green tomatoes underneath. They have a lightly sticky coating on the skin from being protected by the shell, but this rinses right off. They're wonderfully tart and refreshing and a big staple in Mexican and Southwestern cooking.

While tomatillos aren't tomatoes—they're the fruit of a different plant—you'll probably find them near the tomato section in your grocery store. You can also get them at farmers' markets.

This is a delicious dip to enjoy after school or whenever. It's easy to make, and even easier to eat.

Peel the outer layer off the tomatillos and rinse them to get rid of the sticky residue. Cut the tomatillos in half.

Put the tomatillos, avocado, tomatoes, onion, garlic, olive oil, vinegar, and salt in a food processor and blend until creamy. Taste and add a touch more salt if desired.

Serve with tortilla chips.

NOTE

Regular yellow onions can have a strong flavor, so we definitely recommend the sweet onions here.

cheesy panko crisps

MAKES 8 CRACKERS   PREP TIME: 4 minutes   COOK TIME: 7 minutes

½ cup grated sharp Cheddar cheese

1 tablespoon grated Parmesan cheese (fresh is preferable, but canned is fine)

2 tablespoons panko bread crumbs

Strawberry jam or a drizzle of honey for topping (optional)

twin tip

We highly recommend using parchment paper when you're baking, because it makes cleanup quick and easy. Just be sure you don't get parchment paper confused with wax paper, like we once did, because wax paper is not heat-resistant or nonstick if you bake with it. Yes, a sad night when we had to throw away our wax-tasting peanut butter cookies—they were no longer the ultimate.

These crisps are basically cheese and crackers rolled into one. They make a really good quick snack, and we double the recipe if friends are over.

Panko crumbs are a little bigger and crispier than normal bread crumbs. We add them to give the crisps a nice crunch and texture. If you are gluten-free, you can substitute gluten-free panko bread crumbs.

Preheat the oven to 375°F. Line a baking sheet with parchment paper.

In a bowl, mix the Cheddar cheese, Parmesan cheese, and bread crumbs. Fill a tablespoon with the mixture, pressing it down firmly in the spoon.

Drop the tablespoon of mixture onto the baking sheet, pushing any stray cheese and crumbs into the mound. Repeat, continuing to mix the ingredients together as you make each crisp because the panko and Parmesan like to congregate on the bottom of the bowl. You'll wind up with 8 crisps on the baking sheet.

Bake for 7 minutes. Let cool for 3 to 4 minutes before removing the crisps from the baking sheet and serving.

We sometimes add a little dollop of strawberry jam or a drizzle of honey to these because the sweet-and-salty combination is delicious.

spring rolls with sesame ginger dipping sauce

MAKES 4 SPRING ROLLS PREP TIME: 15 TO 20 MINUTES

¼ teaspoon peeled, freshly grated ginger (see Twin Tips, page 115)

1 tablespoon seasoned rice wine vinegar (see Notes, page 62)

1 teaspoon honey

2 tablespoons soy sauce

1 teaspoon toasted sesame oil

SPRING ROLLS

4 spring roll rice wrappers (see Notes, page 62)

4 teaspoons finely chopped cilantro

½ avocado, removed from skin and cut into long, thin strips

½ cup shredded carrot (about half a carrot—the large end)

¼ cup alfalfa sprouts

twin tips

If you don't like cilantro in this recipe or others, you can substitute fresh Italian parsley. We love cilantro, but apparently some people are born not liking it.

By the way, did you know that coriander is dried cilantro? We rarely use coriander, which tastes quite different than fresh cilantro.

You've probably eaten spring rolls at a restaurant, but never thought to make them at home. We hope you do, because these are a simple and fun after-school snack or appetizer for any occasion. The rice paper is really cool because it's hard at first, but when you add the magic of water, it turns into a soft, crepelike wrapper. Emily is a master at these—part patience and part delicate fingers.

We've used our favorite fillings here, but you can make these your own with any of the filling options on page 62.

To make the sauce, place the grated ginger, vinegar, honey, soy sauce, and sesame oil in a bowl and whisk together so the honey is well incorporated. You can make the sauce 2 days ahead of time and store it in the fridge.

To make the spring rolls, make one at a time. Grab a wide mixing bowl and fill halfway with water. Then, following the package directions, dip the first wrapper.

Lay the wrapper out on a flat surface. In the middle of the wrapper, place 1 tablespoon cilantro, a couple strips of avocado, 2 tablespoons of carrot, and 1 tablespoon of sprouts.

To wrap, imagine you are making an envelope. Fold in the bottom so you are slightly overlapping the veggies, then fold the right side, then the left side. Now roll the wrapper upward so it forms a roll.

Repeat until all the spring rolls are done. Enjoy with the dipping sauce. You can make these an hour or two before you enjoy them, but don't refrigerate them because the wrappers will harden again. Just keep them in a container at room temperature until your friends arrive, if you can wait that long.

NOTES

Seasoned rice wine vinegar is a little sweeter than regular rice wine vinegar.

You can buy spring roll wrappers in the Asian food section of the grocery store.

Be patient as you make these, because the wrappers are delicate.

FILLING OPTIONS

For fun, invite friends over and set up a Spring Roll Wrapping Bar. Set out the wrappers, bowls of water, and little bowls or a tray of ingredients that are finely chopped, shredded, or cut into thin strips. Good choices include:

Alfalfa sprouts	Cucumber
Avocado	Edamame
Basil	Lettuce
Cabbage	Mint
Carrot	Red, yellow, or orange bell peppers
Chives	Sesame seeds
Cilantro	Sprouts
Cold cooked rice or rice noodles	Tofu
Cooked shrimp or crab	

You can prep all the ingredients yourself or ask each of your friends to bring a different filling.

crispy lemon & thyme chickpeas

MAKES 2 TO 4 SERVINGS   PREP TIME: 10 minutes   COOK TIME: 15 minutes

2 tablespoons extra-virgin olive oil

One 15-ounce can chickpeas, drained, rinsed, and dried

Salt

2 teaspoons dried thyme

1 teaspoon packed lemon zest (this is the zest from 1 lemon; see Notes, page 135)

2 teaspoons fresh lemon juice

twin tips

Chickpeas are also called garbanzo beans, and they're the main ingredient in hummus.

You can save the liquid from the chickpeas—this is called aquafaba, and it can be used as an egg replacer (see page 15).

We've tried the packaged chickpea snacks from the grocery store, but we prefer our homemade version because it has a better taste and texture. While it sounds a little strange to eat beans with your hands, this is finger food, and we eat it like popcorn.

Speaking of weird snack habits, we love to take lightly salted and chilled chickpeas to school as a snack—they're like little protein poppers.

Select a frying pan and a flat lid that will fit inside the pan, not rest on the edges. You're going to cook the chickpeas with the lid directly on top of them to limit splatter and help crisp up the chickpeas. (The lid acts like a sandwich press.)

Over medium heat, add the oil to the frying pan. When the oil is hot, add the chickpeas and sprinkle ¼ teaspoon of salt over them. Stir to coat the chickpeas in the salt and oil.

Place the lid directly on the chickpeas (they will sizzle and pop) and cook for 4 minutes untouched. Give them a stir and continue cooking them for another 4 minutes, keeping them tucked under the lid.

Remove the lid and sprinkle the chickpeas with the thyme, ½ teaspoon of the lemon zest, and the lemon juice. Gently stir and return the lid for another 4 to 6 minutes, or until the chickpeas have browned and crisped up on several sides.

When the chickpeas are done, put them in a bowl and toss them with the remaining ½ teaspoon lemon zest and a pinch or two of salt to taste. Enjoy warm right away.

moroccan spiced nuts

1 tablespoon ground cinnamon

½ teaspoon ground cumin

¾ teaspoon ground ginger

¾ teaspoon allspice

3 pinches of salt

2 tablespoons coconut oil or extra-virgin olive oil

2 tablespoons light brown sugar

1 cup sliced almonds

¾ cup shelled walnut halves

¾ cup golden raisins

These nuts have a ton of flavor—and if you aren't normally a fan of adding raisins to food, we think this recipe will change your mind. The raisins add a sweetness and texture that complement the spices perfectly. Use the golden raisins if you can, because they're juicier.

In addition to making a great snack, this is a nice gift to give during the holidays.

Preheat the oven to 350°F and line a baking sheet with parchment paper.

Thoroughly mix the cinnamon, cumin, ginger, allspice, and salt in a small bowl.

In a medium saucepan, heat the coconut oil and brown sugar over low heat until the oil melts. As soon as the oil is melted, mix the sugar in well, then turn off the heat and remove the pan from the burner. (Don't overcook the sugar; if you try to totally melt it down, it will clump and caramelize.) Add the almonds, walnut halves, and raisins to the pan and stir to coat them evenly.

Sprinkle the spices over the nuts and raisins and stir until they are evenly coated. Spread the mixture onto the baking sheet and bake for 10 minutes. Let cool and enjoy right away or store in an airtight container for several days.

NOTE

Check out the raisins when they come out of the oven. They blow up like balloons and then deflate again when they cool.

lemony white bean dip

MAKES 4 TO 6 SERVINGS   PREP TIME: 5 minutes

One 15-ounce can white beans (also called cannellini beans), drained and rinsed

2 tablespoons fresh lemon juice

2 tablespoons extra-virgin olive oil, plus more for serving

½ garlic clove, minced

⅛ teaspoon salt

Carrot sticks, sliced yellow or red bell peppers, broccoli or cauliflower florets, and / or tortilla chips for dipping

Give us a can of beans, and we're happy. Okay, that sounds weird, but it's true. We get home from school, whip this up, dig into it, and quickly find ourselves at the bottom of the bowl.

Beans are so versatile that we use them in lots of different ways, from main courses and side dishes to soups and snacks. One go-to for us is this white bean dip, which has just the right touch of lemon and garlic and is especially delicious when we make it with a nice olive oil.

We happen to have a really good batch of olive oil right now that our friends were kind enough to share with us. Their family has an olive tree orchard in Greece, where they make tons of olive oil, and they get a supply of it shipped here.

For one of our birthday parties, we did a food tour and stopped at a local store with a wide variety of olive oils. They let us taste-test olive oils from different countries—such as Greece, Italy, and Spain—they look and taste very different, and they're all good.

Put the beans, lemon juice, olive oil, garlic, and salt in a food processor and blend until smooth and creamy.

Put the dip in a bowl and drizzle a little olive oil on top. Serve with vegetables and tortilla chips.

NOTE

We also use this as a spread on wraps and sandwiches.

oat & date power drops

MAKES 12 DROPS   PREP TIME: 15 minutes

1 cup pitted dried Medjool dates

½ cup shelled walnuts

½ cup old-fashioned rolled oats (not quick oats)

1–2 tablespoons water

24 chocolate chips or butterscotch chips (you can use some of each if you like)

½ cup unsweetened shredded coconut

These have been one of our favorite snacks since we were little. The dates make them sweet, reminding us a little of cookie dough. They're quick to make and require no baking. They are a frequent school snack and one of our main power snacks on game days.

Put the dates, walnuts, and oats in a food processor (with the chop blade) and blend. While the food processor is on, stream in 1 tablespoon of water. Blend until the mixture is all balled up and moist. If it's still dry and crumbly, stream in 1 more tablespoon of water. The mixture should have a consistency like cookie dough.

Carefully remove the blade from the processor.

Take about 1 tablespoon of the "dough" and roll it between your hands to form a ball. (Dip your hands in water before rolling the balls; that way, the mixture won't stick as much and will be easier to roll.) Make an imprint in the middle of the ball and stuff it with your choice of 2 chocolate chips or 2 butterscotch chips (or one of each).

Put the coconut in a bowl and roll each drop to coat it. Store in the fridge for up to 5 days.

NOTE

Even if you buy pitted dates, you should still check them for pits by bending them in the middle. We've occasionally found pits in dates that were supposedly pitted.

chocolate cranberry almond bars

PREP TIME: 20 minutes   COOK TIME: 25 to 30 minutes

1 egg

1 teaspoon vanilla extract

⅓ cup granulated sugar

⅓ cup packed light brown sugar

1 cup unbleached all-purpose flour

1 teaspoon baking soda

1 teaspoon ground cinnamon

¼ teaspoon salt

¼ cup coconut oil, melted

¼ cup smooth, unsweetened applesauce, store-bought or homemade (page 26)

¾ cup creamy, unsweetened almond butter

½ cup dried cranberries

½ cup semisweet chocolate chips

½ cup sliced almonds

These bars are somewhere between a dessert and a health food, so we're calling them a snack because then you are entitled to eat more. They are really filling and get you through a long day. They usually don't last longer than a day around us, but we've realized that this is true for a lot of food in our house.

Preheat the oven to 350°F and line an 8½-inch square metal pan with parchment paper.

Using a stand or hand mixer, mix the egg, vanilla, and granulated and brown sugars until they are an even consistency. In a separate bowl, mix together the flour, baking soda, cinnamon, and salt. Add the dry ingredients to the wet mixture. Add the melted coconut oil, applesauce, and almond butter and mix until combined. Add the cranberries, chocolate chips, and sliced almonds and mix well.

Transfer to the pan and bake for 25 to 30 minutes, or until a knife inserted into the center comes out clean. Let cool for 15 minutes and cut into squares before serving. Store in an airtight container at room temperature for 2 days or in the fridge for 5 days.

twin tip

The almond butter we buy has a lot of oil at the top that needs to be mixed in. When we do this, we put the container in a baggie or on a paper towel because the oil tends to spill out and over.

4

soups, salads & sides

Because we can seem like picky eaters (vegetarian and on-and-off gluten-free, occasionally experimenting with dairy-free), sometimes people are a little nervous when we go to their houses for dinner. But we're actually easy to please, because we're totally happy having soups, salads, and sides as our main dish.

In fact, sides really can be the stars of the table. If you think about it, most people seem to love the sides of Thanksgiving more than the turkey itself.

The side dishes in this chapter are in our constant rotation, and we often turn them into main courses. Soup is on our table about three days a week, no matter the season. What we don't use, we freeze or stir into rice. Salads are refreshing and simple, and the chopping is a calming no-brainer activity. All of the veggie dishes, from Carrot-Potato Mash (page 95) to Decadent Parmesan Zucchini (page 89), are delicious ways to kick up the veggie count for the day.

While we're calling these recipes "sides," eat them any time and any way you want. Turn them into a main course, serve them as an accompaniment, or just make them whenever hunger strikes.

By the way, if we're ever loafing around or in a mood, our mom says, "Why don't you cook something?" It solves everything—and in fact, that's how we came up with many of the recipes in this chapter. So the next time you're bored or feeling down, think of it as an opportunity to create something awesome in the kitchen.

creamy, crunchy tortilla soup

MAKES 6 SERVINGS   PREP TIME: 20 minutes   COOK TIME: 25 minutes

2 tablespoons extra-virgin olive oil

1 medium sweet onion, diced

2 celery stalks, diced

1 peeled, washed carrot, diced (or 8 baby carrots)

1 large zucchini, sliced into quarters

½ teaspoon ground turmeric

½ teaspoon smoked paprika

½ teaspoon ground cumin

½ teaspoon chili powder

½ teaspoon salt

1 medium garlic clove, minced

5 cups vegetable broth

1 cup canned diced or chopped tomatoes in their puree

One 15-ounce can black beans, drained and rinsed

1 cup frozen corn kernels (regular or fire-roasted)

Tortilla chips, store-bought or homemade (recipe follows), chopped avocado, sour cream, hot sauce, cilantro, and/or shredded rotisserie chicken for topping

Limes, quartered, for serving

Our dad is a huge fan of Mexican food, so this is one of his favorite dishes. The combination of the hearty soup, the cool avocado and sour cream toppings, and the crispy tortillas is irresistible.

Don't let the long list of ingredients in this recipe worry you. Soups often have lots of ingredients, but in this case, they're easy to prep.

We usually make this soup the "main event" for a meal, serving a large salad or rice on the side.

Place a large saucepan over medium-low heat and add the oil. Add the onion and celery to the pan and sauté for 8 to 10 minutes, until the vegetables become transparent and the onions begin to caramelize (meaning that they turn a golden brown).

Add the carrot, zucchini, turmeric, smoked paprika, cumin, chili powder, and salt, and sauté for about 5 minutes, until the zucchini start to become transparent.

Add the garlic and stir for 1 minute.

Stir in the vegetable broth, tomatoes, beans, and corn. Bring to a simmer, then cover and cook over medium-low heat for 12 minutes, stirring occasionally.

Remove the pan from the heat and, using an immersion blender, blend until still slightly chunky. If you don't have an immersion blender, add half the soup to a blender, puree until still slightly chunky, and pour it back into the pot. Serve with desired toppings and lime wedges.

→

Homemade Tortilla Chips

MAKES 2 CUPS   PREP TIME: 2 minutes   COOK TIME: 8 minutes

5 corn tortillas

1 tablespoon extra-virgin olive oil

½ teaspoon salt

twin tips

If a recipe calls for several spices that are added at the same time, premeasure the spices and put all of them into one small bowl so you can just dump them in together when the time comes.

If you wind up with a little bit of soup left over that's not enough for a whole serving, you can add it as the "gravy" to a serving of rice.

You can use store-bought tortilla chips, but these are fresher and tastier, and they take just 10 minutes to make.

Preheat the oven to 400°F and grease a baking sheet.

Cut the tortillas into strips 1 to 2 inches long and ¼ inch wide. Place the strips in a bowl and toss them with the olive oil and salt, making sure they are all coated. Place in a single layer on the prepared baking sheet and bake for 8 minutes. Store in an airtight container in the fridge for up to 2 days.

NOTE

Because we add salty tortilla chips to this, the soup itself is less salty. Add more salt if you wish, as always.

chilled cucumber soup

PREP TIME: 15 minutes

1 slice white bread (or any type of bread you want)

1 cup milk

2 English cucumbers, quartered (they measure about 15 inches; see Notes)

3 celery stalks, diced

¼ cup diced sweet onion

¼ cup extra-virgin olive oil, plus more for serving

1 teaspoon salt

¼ cup finely chopped flat-leaf Italian parsley

3–4 cranks of black pepper

Croutons and/or sliced avocado for topping (optional)

This cool soup is light and fresh tasting. If you ever binge on junk food, make this soup afterward because it's like eating spa health food (and it's really good).

While this might seem like a summer dish, it's January 1 as we're writing this—and colder than any other New Year's Day we've experienced—and guess what? We're having this soup! It's refreshing, just like the start of a new year.

Lightly toast the bread.

Add the milk to a blender or food processor. Then add the toasted bread, cucumbers, celery, onion, olive oil, salt, parsley, and pepper. Blend until smooth or slightly chunky. (If you use a blender, you'll get a smoother texture. It'll be a little chunkier if you use a food processor.)

Serve right away with a drizzle of olive oil and toppings, or put in the fridge to chill for a few hours.

NOTES

You can refrigerate this overnight and put it in a jar if you want soup-to-go. Just give it a stir before serving.

You don't need to peel or seed English cucumbers—easy, and one less thing to wash, a peeler!

If you're familiar with gazpacho, a chilled tomato-and-veggie soup, you may know that sometimes it's served creamy and sometimes it's a bit more textured or chunky. It's a matter of preference, just as with this soup. We personally enjoy it creamier.

maple corn bisque

MAKES 6 SERVINGS   PREP TIME: 15 minutes   COOK TIME: 30 minutes

1 sweet onion, diced

3 celery stalks, diced

2 tablespoons extra-virgin olive oil

12 baby carrots, diced (about ⅔ cup)

1 medium unpeeled white or yellow potato, chopped into ½-inch cubes (about 1 cup)

3 cups frozen corn kernels

2½ cups veggie broth

One 13- to 14-ounce can full-fat coconut milk (shake the can well before opening)

1 teaspoon ground turmeric

1 teaspoon salt

⅛ teaspoon freshly ground black pepper

2 pinches of red pepper flakes

¼ cup maple syrup, plus more for serving

Croutons for topping (optional)

We are soup people, because soup is cozy and filling (plus we live in New Jersey, where it gets *cold*). We make this corn bisque the center of a meal, serving it with popovers and salad.

This is another one of our recipes that's a pretty golden color because we add in turmeric, which enhances the flavor and gives the bisque a healthy boost. We've also added another one of our favorite ingredients—maple syrup. We cannot tell you how perfect it makes this soup. (You'll just have to try it for yourself.)

This soup is quite filling, so we often have leftovers. That works out fine for us, because we take it for lunch the next day.

In a large stockpot over medium heat, sauté the onion and celery in the olive oil for 8 to 10 minutes, or until the vegetables are soft and transparent.

Add the carrots, potato, corn, veggie broth, coconut milk, turmeric, salt, pepper, and red pepper flakes, and bring to a simmer. Cover the pot, turn the heat to low, and cook for 15 minutes, or until the carrots and potatoes are soft. (Test the carrots and potatoes with a fork at 15 minutes. If they're still hard, cook, covered, for another 5 minutes.)

Transfer the soup to a blender and blend to the desired consistency. Put the soup back into the pot, add the maple syrup (don't forget—this is a very important ingredient), and stir well. Serve with croutons and an extra drizzle of syrup, if desired.

sweet pea soup

MAKES 4 TO 6 SERVINGS   PREP TIME: 15 minutes   COOK TIME: 10 to 15 minutes

2 tablespoons extra-virgin olive oil

1 medium sweet onion, diced

2 celery stalks, diced

One 13- to 14-ounce can full-fat coconut milk (shake the can well before opening)

3 cups veggie broth

2 cups packed fresh baby spinach

2¼ cups frozen petite sweet peas (the small, petite peas are best)

½ teaspoon salt

5 cranks of black pepper

1 whole ripe pear, cored and chopped (a Bartlett, D'Anjou, or Bosc pear will work)

This is a variation on a soup we made for Rachael Ray. As we mentioned back in the introduction, we made it along with a Sugar Snap Pea Sauce to demonstrate how to enjoy peas in two ways (a play on twins, and we called it Two Peas in a Pod).

We *love* peas. They're sweet, they have a great crunchy texture, and they're a beautiful bright green. In fact, Emily's bedroom is painted this color.

We're crazy about fresh snow peas and sugar snap peas, and we always have a bag of frozen peas that we'll eat right out of the bag (weird but good). The only pea thing we're not fans of is split pea soup—so if you're not a split pea soup fan yourself, don't worry. This soup is totally different; it's light and fresh and has a hint of sweetness from the sweet peas and the fresh pear.

In a large stockpot, heat the olive oil over medium heat and add the onion and celery. Sauté until the vegetables start to become transparent, 5 to 7 minutes. Stir in the coconut milk and broth and mix well.

Turn the heat to high, add the spinach, peas, salt, and pepper, and bring to a simmer. Simmer for only 1 minute, then remove from the heat. The spinach will have just wilted.

Carefully add the soup to a blender. Add the raw pear to the blender and blend until completely smooth and creamy. If this doesn't all fit in your blender at once, blend it in batches.

If desired, add more salt and pepper to taste and serve.

corn off the cob salad

3 ears corn on the cob

1 cup loosely packed basil (about 10 large leaves)

1 cup good cherry tomatoes, quartered (about 15 tomatoes; see Note)

1 cup ¼-inch diced English cucumber

½ cup crumbled feta (or crumbled goat cheese)

3 tablespoons extra-virgin olive oil

Salt and freshly ground black pepper

This salad is simple, and the ingredients are so fresh they don't need much help. You're really just the assembler of awesome garden goodies.

We eat this about twice a week during summer corn season—but if we see corn on the cob in the market any time of year, we grab it to make this recipe.

The only dressing we use for this salad is salt and olive oil, so we think having a good olive oil is extra important. Our favorite is Hojiblanca—an olive oil we receive as a gift each Christmas and are not particularly good at sharing, except when it comes to this salad.

Fill a large stockpot halfway with water and bring to a boil. Add the corn and boil for 8 minutes. Let the corn cool on the counter or stick it in the freezer for about 5 minutes to cool it down.

Using a good knife, hold the corn vertically on a cutting board and cut downward to scrape off the corn kernels. Chiffonade the basil (see page 12 for tips on chiffonading). Add the corn, tomatoes, cucumber, feta, and basil to a large bowl. Drizzle on the olive oil and stir. Sprinkle with salt and pepper to taste and stir. Serve immediately or refrigerate for several hours before serving.

NOTE

You need to use good tomatoes to really get the "summer" in this salad, so if we are buying them from the grocery store in the middle of winter and not getting them from a garden or farmers' market, we use cherry tomatoes because they are the sweetest. The wonderful Kumato tomatoes (see Twin Tip, page 35) come in a cherry size as well as the regular size.

grilled romaine with creamy basil dressing

MAKES 4 SERVINGS   PREP TIME: 20 minutes   COOK TIME: 2 minutes

DRESSING

¼ cup shelled walnuts

½ cup extra-virgin olive oil

¼ cup softened cream cheese (regular, not nonfat)

1 cup packed fresh basil leaves, washed

1 small garlic clove

⅛ teaspoon salt

A few cranks of black pepper

ROMAINE

2 whole hearts romaine (try to get prewashed; if not, wash—leaving the bulb end on—and pat dry thoroughly)

3 tablespoons extra-virgin olive oil

Salt and freshly ground black pepper

GARNISH

¼ cup sliced almonds

¼ cup crumbled feta cheese

Freshly ground black pepper (optional)

The idea of grilling lettuce sounded crazy to us at first, but it works. It adds a cool smokiness to salads.

We came up with this recipe after our mom became obsessed with a grilled chipotle Caesar salad she ordered every time we went to a restaurant in the Adirondacks. We like to serve it with our creamy basil dressing because she's also obsessed with basil.

We live in the Northeast, and while it gets pretty cold, we grill year-round even if there's a little snow on the ground. As far as grilling goes, we're not (yet) in charge of turning the grill on and off, but we've started flipping some stuff. Just sharing, so you know we're not expecting you to be a master griller.

If you don't have a grill—or it's snowing, raining, or too breezy to cook outdoors—we have a perfect alternative: the broiler. You'll find both our grilled version and our broiler version below.

To make the dressing, preheat the oven to 350°F. Place the walnuts on a baking sheet and toast in the oven for 5 minutes. Shake the pan after 2 minutes to make sure the nuts aren't burning on one side. Set them aside to cool a bit. Add the olive oil, cream cheese, cooled walnuts, basil, garlic, salt, and pepper to a blender. Blend on high speed until the ingredients are creamy and the dressing is a beautiful green. You can make this ahead of time and keep it in the fridge for up to 2 days.

For the romaine, evenly slice each heart in half lengthwise. Be careful not to cut off the end/bulb, as you need the leaves to stay together. Baste each side of each half with the olive oil and add a light sprinkling of salt and some pepper.

To grill the romaine, heat a grill to medium and grill the romaine for 1 minute per side (do not leave the grill unattended because you need to remove the romaine quickly). It will get charred in places, but that's the really good part!

To make the romaine using an oven broiler, turn the broiler on high. Place the romaine on a baking sheet and place under the broiler for about 1 minute and 45 seconds. Flip the romaine to the other side and broil for another 1 minute and 45 seconds. (Check on the romaine at the 1-minute mark; if it looks wilted and a little charred, you can flip or take it out then.) Make sure you use tongs when you flip the romaine.

To assemble the salad, put one half of a romaine heart on each plate. Drizzle each with the dressing and sprinkle the sliced almonds and feta on top. Add a few cranks of pepper.

twin tips

Broilers cook food incredibly fast, so remain present whenever you're broiling and set a timer. We say this because all ovens are different.

If you've never tried feta cheese, it's quite tangy and salty and has a strong taste. You can use crumbled goat cheese if you'd like something milder.

asian slaw lettuce cups

MAKES 4 TO 6 SERVINGS   PREP TIME: 25 minutes

DRESSING

2 tablespoons toasted
sesame oil

3 tablespoons extra-virgin
olive oil

2 tablespoons water

1 tablespoon white miso

2 tablespoons lime juice

1 tablespoon honey

1 teaspoon sesame seeds

⅛ teaspoon salt

SALAD

1 cup shredded purple cabbage

2 cups peeled, shredded carrots
(about 2½ peeled carrots)

½ cup shelled sunflower seeds

1 avocado, peeled and diced
into ¼-inch pieces

½ cup canned mandarin
oranges, drained

1 cup ¼-inch diced English
cucumber (about ½ cucumber)

¼ cup packed fresh cilantro,
finely chopped

4–6 large lettuce leaves
(Boston lettuce or iceberg)

Salt and freshly ground
black pepper

This is a really pretty salad that's fun to eat because it's sweet, salty, citrusy, creamy, and crunchy—all in the same bite! As salads go, it's also easy to eat—no trying to stuff huge pieces of lettuce in your mouth. We did add lettuce cups to serve it in because it's kind of fun . . . but we're not saying that you should stuff the whole lettuce cup in your mouth, either.

The dressing contains miso, a thick paste made from soybeans, which adds texture and a rich flavor. If you have miso left over, try dissolving it in water and adding it to vegetable soups—it's delicious.

You can easily transform this recipe into an entrée by adding in pieces of rotisserie chicken, diced cooked shrimp, or tofu. As an entrée, it serves 2 to 3 with some rice on the side.

To make the dressing, add the sesame oil, olive oil, water, miso, lime juice, honey, sesame seeds, and salt to a bowl. Stir vigorously until the miso is thoroughly blended in. Set aside. (You can make this dressing 2 days ahead, and the leftovers will keep for 2 more days.)

To make the salad, toss the cabbage, carrots, sunflower seeds, avocado, mandarin oranges, cucumber, and cilantro together in a large bowl.

Add ¼ cup of the dressing to the salad and toss so everything is coated.

Put 1 lettuce leaf on each plate, topping it with the salad. After plating the salad, sprinkle it lightly with salt and pepper.

crisp chopped salad with honey vinaigrette

MAKES 6 SERVINGS AS AN APPETIZER OR 3 TO 4 SERVINGS AS A ENTRÉE   PREP TIME: 30 minutes

VINAIGRETTE

½ cup extra-virgin olive oil

1 tablespoon red wine vinegar

2 tablespoons balsamic vinegar

1 teaspoon Dijon mustard

1½ teaspoons honey

¼ teaspoon salt

⅛ teaspoon freshly ground black pepper

This is the kind of salad you could eat with a spoon if you wanted to. In fact, we'll grab a cereal bowl and do just that.

We don't eat a lot of iceberg lettuce, but this is a great way to enjoy it because it's crisp and refreshing and goes beautifully with the other veggies. We add capers to this because along with the feta, they add a nice saltiness to the salad.

To make the vinaigrette, put the olive oil, red wine vinegar, balsamic vinegar, mustard, honey, salt, and pepper in a jar and shake or stir vigorously. The vinaigrette can be made ahead and stored in the fridge for 3 to 4 days. Remove from the fridge 20 minutes prior to using.

To make the salad, preheat the oven to 400°F. Spread the pine nuts on a baking sheet and toast for 3 minutes. They burn fast, so don't turn your back on them. Also, don't eat all the pine nuts before they go in the salad! If you're tempted to do this, toast some extras to snack on.

Add the apple, cucumber, lettuce, bell pepper, parsley, chickpeas, capers, feta, and shrimp to a large salad bowl and toss. Set aside ¼ cup of the dressing, and pour the rest of the dressing on the salad. Add salt and pepper to taste, and toss well. Put the extra dressing on the table, should anyone need an extra drizzle.

CHOPPED SALAD

¼ cup pine nuts

1 apple, diced into ¼-inch pieces (we like Fuji or Crispin)

½ English cucumber, diced into ¼-inch pieces

½ head iceberg lettuce, diced into ¼-inch pieces

1 bell pepper (yellow, orange, or red), diced into ¼-inch pieces

½ cup packed chopped flat-leaf Italian parsley

One 15- to 16-ounce can chickpeas, drained and rinsed

3 tablespoons capers, strained

¾ cup crumbled feta cheese

6–8 grilled or cooked shrimp, chopped, or 1 cup shredded rotisserie chicken (optional)

Salt and freshly ground black pepper

NOTE

If you want a feta swap, use crumbled goat cheese. This will create a smothered/creamy effect when you toss your salad.

twin tips

Capers are the unripe flower buds from a bush that grows in the Mediterranean and the Middle East. They're brined and have a salty, lemony flavor.

A *vinaigrette* is basically just a dressing you make by mixing oil (preferably extra-virgin olive oil) with something acidic (for instance, vinegar or lemon juice) and adding spices or seasonings. Once you've mastered one vinaigrette, you can make dozens and dozens of variations, so this is a great basic chef skill to learn.

decadent parmesan zucchini

2 tablespoons extra-virgin olive oil

1 sweet onion, diced

2 zucchini (if small, use 3 or 4), sliced into ¼-inch-thick half-moons

1 teaspoon salt

¼ teaspoon freshly ground black pepper

2 small to medium garlic cloves, minced

2 tablespoons freshly grated Parmesan cheese

You probably don't hear the words *decadent* and *zucchini* used together often. But this dish is sinfully good!

Zucchini was one of the first vegetables we got hooked on, because when it's cooked well and softens, it just melts in your mouth. We've always liked zucchini and Parm together, in everything from zucchini boats to roasted zucchini—but this recipe, in which we sauté the squash, is our true favorite.

Heat the oil in a medium-large frying pan over medium heat. Add the diced onion and sauté until translucent (meaning see-through). This will take 5 to 7 minutes.

Once the onion is translucent, add the sliced zucchini to the pan. Sprinkle with the salt and pepper and sauté for another 10 to 15 minutes, stirring occasionally, until the zucchini starts to soften, becomes translucent, and is cooked through. Add the garlic and cook for about 5 minutes, stirring regularly so the garlic does not burn. All of the veggies should be very soft and almost a creamy consistency. We intentionally cook the zucchini beyond "done" because that's what makes them decadent.

Remove the veggies from the sauté pan and put them in a serving bowl. Add the Parmesan cheese and stir so the cheese thoroughly coats the veggies. Grab your serving fast, because this will not last long.

NOTE

Watch the timing on your onions and zucchini. If your pan is smaller, they'll take longer to soften and cook because they are crowded.

maple roasted carrots

PREP TIME: 5 minutes   COOK TIME: 40 minutes

One 16-ounce bag baby carrots

1 tablespoon extra-virgin olive oil

1 tablespoon maple syrup

¼ teaspoon salt

⅛ teaspoon freshly ground black pepper

twin tips

Maple syrup baked onto surfaces can be difficult to clean up. We soak any stubborn spots with Bartender's Friend. We also cook on parchment, which makes cleanup easy.

When a recipe calls for maple syrup, make sure you're using the real thing. Don't use pancake syrup, which is mainly corn sugar and artificial ingredients. Real maple syrup is more expensive than pancake syrup, but it's worth it.

These carrots barely hit the table because we eat them like finger food. They're a no-brainer veggie side because they're good hot, cold, or at room temperature. You can use whole carrots for this as well, but we've gotten in the quick habit of just grabbing a bag of baby carrots and whipping this up.

By the way, maple syrup is a natural fit for roasting pretty much any veggie, so this is something you can experiment with.

Preheat the oven to 400°F and grease a baking sheet or line with parchment paper.

Put the carrots in a bowl and toss with the olive oil, maple syrup, salt, and pepper.

Place the carrots in a single layer on the baking sheet and bake for 40 minutes, turning a couple of times as they cook. Remove them from the oven, let them cool for 5 minutes, and enjoy!

sweet potato fries with southwestern mayo

MAKES 2 SERVINGS   PREP TIME: 15 minutes   COOK TIME: 20 to 25 minutes

FRIES

1 large sweet potato

1½ tablespoons extra-virgin olive oil

¼ teaspoon salt

¼ teaspoon freshly ground black pepper

½ teaspoon chili powder

SOUTHWESTERN MAYO

½ cup mayonnaise or plain full-fat yogurt

2 tablespoons ketchup

1 tablespoon sriracha hot sauce

Pinch of salt

1 teaspoon smoked paprika

½ garlic clove, minced

twin tip

Sweet potatoes are very hard to cut through. When you're cutting a sweet potato, it's easiest to cut it in half and then continue to slice it with the flat parts always flush with the cutting board. That way, it's stable.

Sweet potato fries are hugely popular at restaurants, and they're totally simple to make at home. We like these even better than regular French fries, because the sweet potatoes have more flavor and the chili powder perfects them.

We pair these with our Southwestern Mayo and serve them as a side or make them for a snack. The fries and dip are simple to throw together and make us full and happy. The Southwestern Mayo can be made ahead of time and stored in the fridge for 2 days.

Preheat the oven to 425°F and grease a baking sheet.

To make the fries, peel the sweet potato. Cut it into 1-inch slabs, and then cut the slabs into fry-size pieces ¼ to ½ inch wide.

Add the fries to a bowl and toss them with the olive oil until they're completely coated. Add the salt, pepper, and chili powder and toss again (we use tongs to do this).

Place the fries in a single layer on the baking sheet and bake for 20 to 25 minutes, tossing every 5 minutes. They should be soft and nicely roasted, but not burned. While the fries are cooking, make the mayo.

To make the mayo, combine the mayonnaise, ketchup, sriracha, salt, paprika, and garlic in a small bowl and mix until blended. Serve the fries immediately with the mayo mixture.

twice-baked potatoes

These potatoes are really easy to make, even though they take a while to bake. They're rich and creamy—perfect comfort food.

We used to make baked potatoes the traditional way, and it was a big chore to spread all the different toppings and mash in all the ingredients. Now we simply cream everything together, and the result is perfectly melted and moist and way better.

These twice-baked potatoes have an unexpected ingredient—applesauce. We add applesauce to these because we've always liked it in regular baked potatoes. And we're fans of cheese slices with apple and potato pancakes with applesauce, so it's a natural combo. Trust us.

We normally make these potatoes with just Cheddar cheese and chives on top, but you can customize with the toppings of your choice.

POTATOES

2 medium baking potatoes (for instance, russet)

2–3 teaspoons extra-virgin olive oil

⅛ teaspoon salt

FILLING

2 tablespoons half-and-half (or whole milk)

3 tablespoons good salted butter (we love Kerrygold Irish butter, but any butter is fine)

3 tablespoons freshly grated Parmesan cheese

½ cup smooth, unsweetened applesauce, store-bought or homemade (page 26)

1 tablespoon finely chopped chives

⅛ teaspoon salt

A few cranks of black pepper

4 teaspoons shredded sharp Cheddar cheese

4 teaspoons finely chopped fresh chives (see Twin Tips)

twin tips

You can use kitchen scissors instead of a knife to cut your chives into small pieces.

If you happen to slice open your potatoes before they are done (we have done this), just rest a piece of foil on top of them and bake for another 10 to 20 minutes.

To make the potatoes, preheat the oven to 425°F. Wash and dry the potatoes and prick each one several times with a fork; otherwise, they could explode. Coat the potatoes with the olive oil, put them on a baking sheet, and sprinkle them with salt.

Bake for 1 hour. Check the potatoes to see if they are done. You should be able to slide a sharp knife through to the center. If the knife resists or the potato feels hard, give it another 10 minutes and then check again.

When the potatoes are done, remove the baking sheet from the oven. Using tongs, transfer the potatoes to a cutting board. Using a serrated knife, slice each potato lengthwise, evenly down the middle.

To make the filling, scoop out the insides of the 4 potato halves and transfer to a bowl, leaving a little of the potato to line the skins so they don't get too flimsy. Add the half-and-half, butter, Parmesan cheese, applesauce, chives, salt, and pepper to the bowl. Using a hand mixer, blend until the butter is melted and the potatoes are smooth and creamy. You don't want a lot of chunks, but don't overblend because it will make the potatoes starchy.

To assemble the potatoes, refill the potato halves with the creamy potato mix. Top each potato half with 1 teaspoon of the Cheddar cheese and 1 teaspoon of the chives. Using tongs, carefully place the potatoes back on the baking sheet and bake for another 15 minutes. Let the potatoes cool slightly (about 5 minutes), top with any additional toppings below if you wish, then serve.

TOPPING OPTIONS

Apples, sliced

Flaked sea salt

Greek yogurt

Parsley, finely chopped

Red onion, finely chopped

Sour cream

Tomatoes, chopped

carrot-potato mash

MAKES 4 SERVINGS   PREP TIME: 10 minutes   COOK TIME: 20 to 30 minutes

10 cups water

¾ teaspoon salt

Two 16-ounce bags baby carrots

2 large red potatoes (or 4 small), washed and cut into 1-inch chunks

⅔ cup canned full-fat coconut milk (shake the can well before opening)

¾ teaspoon ground nutmeg

4 teaspoons maple syrup

twin tip

Don't overblend purees containing potatoes, because it will make the potatoes too starchy.

This is a great side dish to make any time, but in our house it's always on the Thanksgiving table because the nutmeg and maple are classic fall flavors.

We use bags of baby carrots because it eliminates peeling and chopping; you don't need to peel the potatoes, either. (We're big on shortcuts.)

Coconut milk adds a creamy texture, but don't worry—it won't taste like coconut. The flavor is mild and simply complements and enhances the other ingredients.

To a large stockpot, add the water and ½ teaspoon of the salt and bring to a boil. Carefully add the carrots and potatoes to the boiling water. (It will splash if you just throw in the veggies, so use a slotted spoon to place them in the water.)

Boil the vegetables for 20 minutes. Test a carrot and a potato and make sure they are soft. You want to be able to stick a fork through both easily.

Strain the veggies (be careful, the pot will be hot and heavy). If you are using an immersion blender, put the carrots and potatoes back in the pot and add the remaining ¼ teaspoon salt, coconut milk, and nutmeg and blend until creamy (a few chunks are good). If not, add all of these ingredients to a food processor and blend, or use a hand mixer to blend them.

Serve a dollop of the puree on each plate, making a little cavity in the middle of each dollop. Drizzle a teaspoon of maple syrup into the cavity, allowing it to run down the sides (kind of like gravy).

broccoli tempura

Vegetable oil for frying

¾ cup unbleached all-purpose flour

¼ cup panko bread crumbs

1½ tablespoons sesame seeds

¾ cup club soda, plus extra if needed

3 cups fresh broccoli florets

Soy sauce or Sesame Ginger Dipping Sauce (page 60)

Tempura is always a treat when we dine out at an Asian restaurant, but we didn't realize how easy it was to make at home until we tried it. We've used all sorts of vegetables, but broccoli is our favorite. Feel free to try other veggies, like green beans, cauliflower, or bell peppers.

Also, the next time you dine out at an Asian restaurant, ask for a bunch of the wooden chopsticks to take home with you. (Or pick some up at your grocery store.) It takes a little practice, but they are fun to master.

In a large stockpot, add 2 to 3 inches of vegetable oil and heat for 5 minutes on medium heat. (It's best to use a large pot here, because then the oil will spatter less.)

Meanwhile, in a medium bowl, combine the flour, bread crumbs, and sesame seeds. Stir together. Pour in the club soda and stir with a fork to incorporate.

Using tongs, dunk 3 to 4 broccoli florets in the batter. Make sure each piece is totally covered in batter. (Have a separate pair of long tongs handy for turning the florets in the oil and removing them.)

Lightly shake the broccoli to get rid of excess batter, and add the battered florets to the hot oil. Cook for about 3 minutes, occasionally turning the florets with the second pair of tongs. After they are a deep golden brown, remove one and cut it open. If there is still wet batter, return and cook 1 more minute.

Continue cooking the florets in batches, placing each cooked batch on a paper towel-lined plate. If your oil gets too hot and the broccoli looks like it's burning, just turn down the heat a bit.

If the batter is looking dry, add another tablespoon or two of the club soda.

Serve these warm with soy sauce for dipping.

NOTES

Don't crowd too many florets in the oil. You want them to have a little "bounce around" space so they cook better.

We tried this with oat flour (see Twin Tip, page 142), and it worked. Also, if you want to make this gluten-free, use gluten-free panko bread crumbs. It doesn't get as golden, but it's still delicious.

The type of oil matters here, so stick with vegetable oil for frying these.

What to do with the used oil? We let it cool for a day and then stick it in a recycled jar or yogurt container and dispose of it in the outdoor garbage.

entrées

When we appeared on *Chopped Junior*, our entrée basket included scallops, chickpea chips, watercress, and—surprise!—birthday cake. It was a fun challenge, but neither one of us ever, *ever* wants to make an entrée with birthday cake again. Luckily for you, we won't throw any strange ingredients like that at you. You'll see many foods you already enjoy, and we think you'll be excited by the new tastes you'll discover.

As you make these recipes, feel free to change things up to suit your own tastes or those of your friends and family. We do this all the time, because we cater to many different food preferences in our own circle. We're vegetarians, our mom is a pescatarian (meaning that she eats fish but not meat or chicken), our dad is a meat-eater, and we have friends with various reasons for avoiding certain foods. So we always try to offer options at home and here.

The good thing is that our recipes can be adapted to make everyone happy. For instance, if we have meat-eaters over, we might suggest ground beef as an optional topping in our rice bowl recipe (page 124). Or we might put tofu on the side rather than in a dish if people aren't sure they want to try it, although many of them wind up being surprised at how good our maple tofu is (page 114). Similarly, if a friend can't eat a certain food, we'll simply substitute another. Cooking is a very flexible art, and we hope you'll see how easy it is to accommodate special eating styles and be more creative in the process.

Whether you stick to these recipes or give them your own twist, you'll find something in this chapter for any occasion. Some of these recipes, like Creamy Polenta with Eggs and Bacon (page 122), are just right for a casual family dinner. Others, like our Pot of Gold Risotto (page 105) or Mediterranean Stuffed Peppers (page 129), are dishes you can serve at the fanciest dinner party—but they're perfect for everyday meals as well. And each one is loaded with fresh, healthy ingredients, so you can feel good about eating and serving them. Enjoy!

pumpkin wonton raviolis

SAUCE

⅓ cup shelled walnuts

1 tablespoon unsalted butter

1 tablespoon extra-virgin olive oil

2 large shallots, chopped

¾ cup milk

2 tablespoons maple syrup

⅛ teaspoon salt

A few cranks of black pepper

FILLING

2 cups canned pumpkin (plain, not the seasoned, sweetened kind made for pie filling)

1⅓ cups full-fat ricotta cheese

½ teaspoon ground nutmeg

½ teaspoon ground cinnamon

¼ teaspoon salt

Several cranks of black pepper

48 wonton wrappers

1 egg, beaten (it's called an egg wash, we don't know why)

Ground cinnamon

Ground nutmeg

We used to buy pumpkin ravioli, but we thought the filling got lost in the pasta. Now we make our own version with extra filling.

We use wonton wrappers for these, so they're super simple to assemble. You'll find wonton wrappers in the refrigerated section of the grocery store. Usually we find them in the produce section—strange, but they must have a reason to put them there! The wontons have a light, silky texture, while the creamy sauce clings to the raviolis and complements the pumpkin flavor perfectly.

We recommend enjoying this recipe year-round, not just when pumpkin is in season.

To make the sauce, preheat the oven to 350°F. Spread the walnuts on a baking sheet and bake for 5 minutes. Set aside.

Meanwhile, in a small skillet set over medium-low heat, melt the butter with the olive oil. Add the chopped shallots and sauté for 3 to 5 minutes, or until the shallots are transparent and just browning. Transfer the shallots and pan drippings to a blender.

Add the toasted walnuts, the milk, the maple syrup, and the salt and pepper to the blender and blend until smooth and creamy.

To make the filling, mix the pumpkin, ricotta, nutmeg, cinnamon, salt, and pepper in a bowl.

→

twin tips

Wonton wrappers are thin and stick together, so make sure you just put one down at a time.

You can make the sauce to go with anything else you can think of or stir leftover sauce into rice.

To assemble the ravioli, place a sheet of parchment paper on each of 2 large baking sheets. Spray the sheets lightly with cooking spray.

Put 12 wonton wrappers on each sheet. In the middle of each wrapper, place a dollop (about 1½ tablespoons) of pumpkin filling, so they are all approximately equal (this doesn't need to be perfect).

On the outside perimeter of each wonton, brush on a little egg wash. Top each wonton with another wonton wrapper, and then, using your fingers, seal the edges. Press down so the top adheres to the egg-washed bottom edges. If pumpkin oozes out, just tuck it in. You're not boiling these, so they'll be fine.

Brush the top of each wonton with a light coating of the egg wash and then sprinkle with a light dusting of cinnamon and nutmeg. (This works best if you use a fine-mesh sieve, such as you'd use for sprinkling on confectioners' sugar.)

Transfer to the oven and bake for 12 minutes, until golden brown. Serve with the sauce. You can eat the raviolis with a fork and knife or pick them up with your fingers and dunk them in the sauce.

You can make the pumpkin filling and the sauce ahead of time and keep them in the fridge for up to 2 days. This makes assembly extra-easy.

pot of gold risotto

5½ cups veggie broth

1½ teaspoons saffron threads

2 shallots, finely chopped

2 celery stalks, finely chopped

6 tablespoons unsalted butter

2 cups Arborio rice

1 tablespoon white wine vinegar

⅓ cup good-quality shredded Parmesan

Salt and freshly ground black pepper

Pea shoots, other sprouts, or chopped Italian parsley for topping (optional)

twin tip

For an authentic risotto, be sure to use the right rice. The rice in risotto needs to absorb lots of liquid and still be al dente (that is, a little firm), and Arborio is an excellent choice for the job. (We've also had good luck with Botan, the rice we use for sushi.) It's not the end of the world if you use regular rice, but the rice won't have the "bite" that's a hallmark of classic risotto.

Most chefs call this risotto milanese, but we prefer our name because the finished dish is a rich gold color. If you like rice—and who doesn't?—then you will be crazy about this! It gets its color from saffron threads, which come from a flower and are very exotic. Saffron is expensive, but we found it at Trader Joe's for about $6 for a 0.70 gram jar, which is all you need.

We made this dish for hundreds of people at the International Home and Housewares Show in Chicago, as well as for a TV program there, and it was a hit. Most risotto milanese recipes call for wine, and obviously each chef has a favorite way to make risotto, but given our age, we swapped the wine for vinegar and you can't tell the difference (so we are told).

In a large saucepan, add the broth and saffron and cook over medium-low heat for 20 minutes so the saffron steeps in the broth. No need to simmer or boil the broth; it is just heated. At the end of this gentle cooking time, the broth will have absorbed the flavor of the saffron.

In a large saucepan or frying pan over medium-low heat, sauté the shallots and celery in the butter until translucent, 3 to 4 minutes (be careful not to burn your shallots). Add the rice and the vinegar and stir until the liquid is absorbed.

Add 1 cup of broth (including the saffron threads) to the rice, constantly stirring until the broth is absorbed. Continue to add more broth, 1 cup at a time, each time waiting for the broth to be absorbed. Do this until all the broth and saffron are added, the rice is tender, and all the broth is absorbed (about 30 minutes). Stir in the Parmesan cheese, season with salt and pepper, add toppings, and serve.

blue cheese turkey burgers

MAKES 4 SERVINGS   PREP TIME: 15 minutes   COOK TIME: 16 minutes

1 pound ground turkey

¾ cup crumbled blue cheese

¼ cup mayonnaise (use Hellmann's Real mayonnaise if you can get it)

⅛ teaspoon salt

⅛ teaspoon freshly ground black pepper

1 tablespoon vegetable oil or enough cooking spray to coat your pan

4 hamburger buns (optional)

4 leaves green-leaf or iceberg lettuce

1 Bermuda onion, sliced

Ketchup for serving

4 tomato slices

We spend our summers with our grandmother, whom we call "GrandMolly" (her name is Molly). She is a foodie like us, but a very different kind of foodie. For example, she has potato chip days. What are those, you wonder? Well, they are the days she allows herself to eat potato chips. She loves potato chips so much she says she has to set aside certain days for them so they remain special.

As for our food differences, GrandMolly enjoys meat and says she can't imagine not eating meat. When we're at her house cooking vegetarian dishes, she's always in the kitchen peering over our shoulders and wondering what in the world we are making. Then, when we finish a recipe, she says she can't get over how delicious it looks.

Even though we're vegetarians and GrandMolly is not, she is one of our best taste-testers. If a recipe passes the "GrandMolly" test, we know the universe will like it.

GrandMolly has tasted many of the recipes in our cookbook, and we wanted to share one of hers as well. This turkey burger recipe is one of her favorites, and together with her, we discussed including the blue cheese. Blue cheese is a taste we did not like ourselves when we were younger, but now we do (especially on cold, crisp lettuce).

Our dad is a huge fan of this recipe. He will usually cook up these burgers when we're out for the night, and it's one of his dad meal nights (burger, chips, pickles, and the TV tuned to the Yankees, Bills, or Sabres).

→

GrandMolly insists on using Hellman's Real mayonnaise for this recipe. However, if you can't get it, you can substitute another full-fat mayonnaise . . . just don't tell her.

While we don't eat meat, we have many family members who do—and they all agree that this simple recipe has a ton of flavor.

Place the turkey, blue cheese, mayonnaise, salt, and pepper in a large bowl and mix with your hands until blended. Do not pack down. Shape the mixture into 4 patties.

Add the oil to a cold frying pan. Turn the heat to medium. Wait half a minute or so before adding the burgers.

Cook the burgers, flipping them when they are browned on the bottom. This will take approximately 7 to 8 minutes. Cook for 7 to 8 more minutes on the other side. If the pan seems dry, add a little cold water. You can do this more than once.

Be sure not to skimp on the cooking, because turkey burgers need to be cooked all the way through. (You do not want them medium-rare.) Your burgers should reach an internal temperature of 180°F on an instant-read thermometer. If you don't have a meat thermometer and you aren't sure if the burgers are done, just make a little slit in one and peek inside. It should look cooked through, with the color and texture inside similar to the outside. You can always put it back in the pan to cook longer.

Transfer the patties to buns and top each one with the lettuce, sliced onion, ketchup, and tomatoes.

NOTES

You can use more or less mayonnaise and blue cheese if desired.

Place a splatter guard on top of the pan when cooking the burgers, or a lid that covers about three-quarters of the pan.

parmesan-crusted grilled cheese

MAKES 1 SANDWICH   PREP TIME: 10 minutes   COOK TIME: 10 minutes

2 slices bread

1 tablespoon mayonnaise

2 tablespoons grated Parmesan cheese

1 teaspoon unsalted butter or nonstick spray

4–6 slices sharp Cheddar cheese (or any other cheese you like)

¼ avocado, sliced into slivers

When we were little, our family made pressed grilled cheese sandwiches all the time. We're adding a new twist to make them extra-crispy on the outside.

We recently submitted this as our signature sandwich to one of our favorite cafés in town, Lillipies. They designated us as the "celebrities" of the month, with our sandwich featured and 10 percent of all proceeds going to SAVE Animal Shelter (where our cats, Sapphire and Pearl, came from).

Spread one side of each slice of bread with mayonnaise, then sprinkle the grated Parmesan onto the mayo side of the bread and press it down so the cheese sticks to the bread.

Melt the butter in a small frying pan over medium heat. Add one slice of the bread to the pan, mayo-and-Parmesan-side down. Let this get golden brown and toasty, then remove to a plate.

Add the other slice of bread to the pan, mayo-and-Parmesan-side down. Lay the Cheddar cheese and slices of avocado on top of the cheese, then cover with the other slice of grilled bread.

Place the top of a saucepan on top of the sandwich and press down lightly, but don't squish out the avocado! Cook until all your cheese is melted.

southwestern chicken (or not!) casserole

MAKES 6 SERVINGS   PREP TIME: 20 minutes (includes cooking the quinoa)   COOK TIME: 25 minutes

2 cups dry quinoa (when cooked, this will make 6 cups)

1 tablespoon taco seasoning, store-bought or homemade (recipe follows)

1½ cups shredded precooked rotisserie chicken (optional)

One 15-ounce jar salsa

Two 15-ounce cans black beans, drained and rinsed

2 cups frozen corn (we love roasted corn—try it if you can find it)

3 cups shredded sharp Cheddar cheese

Diced avocado, chopped cilantro, shredded iceberg lettuce, sour cream, and / or crumbled tortilla chips for topping

We mentioned earlier that it's easy to be flexible when you're cooking for different tastes, and this is a recipe that proves our point. We make the meat-free version, while some of our friends prefer to add the chicken. It works either way, so do what makes you happy. (But even if you are a meat-eater, try the vegetarian version at least once. We think you'll actually like it better.)

Preheat the oven to 350°F and grease an 8 by 11-inch glass or ceramic casserole dish with a lid.

Cook the quinoa according to package directions, adding the taco seasoning to the cooking liquid (this will flavor your quinoa).

When the quinoa is finished, put it in a large bowl and mix in the chicken, salsa, black beans, corn, and 1½ cups of the cheese.

Put the quinoa mix into the casserole dish and sprinkle the remaining 1½ cups of cheese on top.

Bake for 15 minutes with the lid on. Then remove the lid and bake for another 5 to 7 minutes, until the cheese is melted and bubbly. Serve with avocado, cilantro, lettuce, sour cream, and chips for topping.

NOTE

If you don't have a fitted lid for your casserole dish, use aluminum foil, but tent it a bit so it doesn't end up with the cheese sticking to it.

taco seasoning

MAKES 6 TABLESPOONS

3 tablespoons chili powder

1 tablespoon salt

¾ teaspoon garlic powder

¾ teaspoon onion powder

1½ teaspoons smoked paprika

1 tablespoon plus ½ teaspoon ground cumin

Keep this spice mix on hand. You'll have an easy go-to seasoning blend the next time you make this casserole. You can also use this seasoning on eggs, sprinkle it on rice or nachos, stir it into guacamole or sour cream, or mix it with softened butter for a smoky butter.

Mix all the ingredients together in a small bowl and store in a sealed container (we use recycled jam jars). This will keep for months stored in a dry place with other spices.

margherita flatbread pizzas

FLATBREAD

1½ cups unbleached all-purpose flour, plus more for dusting

¾ cup water

2 teaspoons extra-virgin olive oil

½ cup pizza sauce

8 slices (16 ounces) fresh mozzarella, broken into ½-inch pieces (we prefer BelGioioso brand)

8 small tomatoes, sliced

½ cup basil, chopped chiffonade-style (see page 12)

Dried oregano (optional)

Red pepper flakes (optional)

You can buy flatbreads—but why do that when it's so easy to make them from scratch? You can get as creative as you want with the toppings. Try our version here, or add any sort of toppings you like—pesto, ricotta, and tomato, or cheese and pepperoni, you name it.

To make the flatbread, in a medium bowl, combine the flour and water and mix until the mixture has a doughlike texture. It will be sticky.

With floured hands, split the dough into 4 equal parts and place on a well-floured surface, sprinkling additional flour on top of each piece of dough. With a rolling pin, roll out each piece into a flat disk. Add more flour to the surface if needed to keep it from sticking. The dough should be about ¼ inch thick. The shape does not need to be perfect.

Preheat the oven to 350°F.

Heat a medium skillet over medium heat and add about ½ teaspoon of the olive oil. Add the first flatbread and cook for 3 to 4 minutes per side, until it is lightly toasted and the dough is cooked through. Cook the remaining flatbreads, adding ½ teaspoon of olive oil to the pan each time. (You can make the flatbreads ahead of time; they will keep for a few days in the fridge and 1 month in the freezer. Layer them between sheets of wax or parchment paper if you freeze them.)

Place the flatbreads on a baking sheet. Add 1 to 2 tablespoons of pizza sauce to each, then top with the mozzarella, tomatoes, basil, and a sprinkle of oregano and red pepper flakes. Bake for 8 minutes and serve warm.

forbidden rice with maple tofu and carrot-ginger dressing

MAKES 4 TO 6 SERVINGS   PREP TIME: 40 minutes   COOK TIME: 30 minutes

MAPLE TOFU

2 blocks extra-firm tofu,
14 ounces each

2 tablespoons soy sauce

¼ cup maple syrup

FORBIDDEN RICE

2 cups Thai forbidden rice

3 cups canned full-fat coconut milk (shake the cans well before opening)

1 cup water

½ teaspoon salt

CARROT-GINGER DRESSING

1 tablespoon peeled, freshly grated ginger (see Twin Tips)

6 carrots, peeled and quartered, or 36 baby carrots

2 tablespoons apple cider vinegar

1 tablespoon honey

1 tablespoon sesame oil

2 teaspoons soy sauce

¼ cup vegetable oil or canola oil

2 tablespoons rice vinegar

Sliced avocado, cilantro, or parsley for topping

In ancient China, this beautiful black rice was reserved for royalty. Luckily, it's not forbidden to us today! It has a delicious nutty flavor, and it turns a deep purple when you cook it.

This recipe is actually three recipes rolled into one. The recipes work beautifully together, but we also make each one alone. We enjoy the dressing as a dip, we eat the tofu as a finger-food snack, and the coconut rice is a staple side dish of ours.

Tofu is a fun ingredient because it's a blank canvas that lends itself to many different flavors. If this is your first attempt at cooking or eating tofu, we think you'll enjoy the sweet-and-salty twist we give it with maple syrup and soy sauce.

We like this recipe so much that when the food writer for the *Philadelphia Inquirer* interviewed us and asked us to share a recipe, this is the one we picked.

To make the tofu, preheat the oven to 375°F. Grease a baking sheet or line with parchment paper.

Open and drain the tofu. To drain it, place it between several layers of paper towels. (Be sure to put paper towels on top of the tofu as well as under it.) Place a cutting board on top and then a heavy object on top of that (we put our coffee pot on it). Water will drain out of the tofu and be absorbed by the paper towels. Drain for 30 minutes or more.

Remove the tofu and cut into 1-inch squares.

In a bowl, combine the soy sauce and maple syrup and mix. Add the tofu and gently toss to coat. Place the tofu on the baking sheet and bake, flipping twice, until the tofu browns, about 30 minutes. While the tofu is baking, make the rice.

To make the rice, combine the rice, coconut milk, water, and salt in a saucepan. Bring to a boil, stir, reduce the heat to a low simmer, and cover. Cook until the rice is tender and the liquid is absorbed, about 30 minutes. When the rice is done, remove it from the heat and let it stand for 5 minutes before serving.

To make the dressing, process the ginger, carrots, apple cider vinegar, honey, sesame oil, soy sauce, vegetable oil, and rice vinegar in a food processor. Puree until smooth.

Divide the rice among bowls and top with the tofu, avocado slices, and carrot-ginger dressing. Add cilantro or parsley.

twin tips

To save time, process whole, peeled ginger roots in your food processor and store the paste flattened out in a plastic zip-top bag in the freezer. That way, you can simply break off pieces to use in your recipes. Easy!

There are two types of sesame oil—toasted and not. The toasted version is quite dark in color and has a very strong toasty flavor (stating the obvious). The non-toasted is more of a yellowish color. You can use either type in this recipe; they are both really good. If you use the toasted version, it will be a dominant flavor.

zucchini & squash galette

MAKES 4 TO 6 SERVINGS

PREP TIME: 30 minutes (includes sautéing the vegetables)   COOK TIME: 25 minutes

FILLING

1 tablespoon extra-virgin olive oil

2 medium zucchini, sliced ⅛ inch thick and cut into half-moons

1 small yellow squash, sliced ⅛ inch thick and cut into half-moons

1 teaspoon salt

⅛ teaspoon freshly ground black pepper

SAUCE

¼ cup heavy whipping cream or half-and-half

2 teaspoons Dijon mustard

3 tablespoons shredded Parmesan cheese

CRUST

1¼ cups unbleached all-purpose flour, plus more for rolling

½ teaspoon salt

½ cup unsalted butter, cold and cut into small pieces

¼ cup ice-cold water

Galette is a French word that sounds fancy, but don't let that scare you. Basically, it's a free-form pie that doesn't require a pie dish. Galettes are fun to make because they don't need to be perfect, and you can be a little artistic in laying out your filling and molding your dough around it. We enjoy this for dinner or serve it as an appetizer, slicing it into smaller wedges.

We've tweaked our galettes along the way, adding herbs to our sauces and crusts, but when we enjoyed a friend's galette with a mustard sauce, that was the magic we needed! It's delicious—just remember to drizzle some of it on the top before serving.

This recipe has several steps, but don't let that stop you from trying it if you're a beginner, because it's quite simple. You can make the dough for the crust a day ahead if you wish, and store it in the fridge. It makes a fun gift, too; we give our friends dough balls and attach this recipe so they can make their own galettes!

To make the filling, heat the oil in a large saucepan. When it's warm, add the zucchini, yellow squash, salt, and pepper. Sauté until the slices are slightly softened and becoming translucent, 10 to 15 minutes. Set aside until you're ready to add the filling.

To make the sauce, whisk the cream, Dijon, and Parmesan together in a small bowl.

To make the crust, preheat the oven to 425°F and grease a baking sheet. In a food processor, combine the flour and salt and pulse to blend. Add the butter and blend. While the food processor is on, slowly add the water until the dough is blended and clumps.

COATING

1 egg, beaten

2 tablespoons shredded Parmesan cheese

Gather the dough into a ball and place it on a lightly floured sheet of parchment paper. Sprinkle some flour on top and roll out the dough until it is somewhat round and about ¼ to ½ inch thick. Transfer the dough to the prepared baking sheet. (To make rolling and transferring even easier, place another piece of parchment on top so the dough is sandwiched. This keeps the dough from sticking to your rolling pin.)

To assemble the galette, use a spoon to drizzle 2 to 3 tablespoons of the sauce around the dough, leaving about 1½ inches of dough around the edge free of sauce. (Think of your sauce like red sauce on a pizza; you want to taste it, but it's not the star of the show.) Reserve the leftover sauce for serving.

Next, add the zucchini and yellow squash. Starting at the center of the dough, layer the zucchini and squash in a flower petal-like pattern going outward, slightly overlapping the slices. Layer the vegetables until you reach the edge of your sauce.

Now, using a spatula, flip the outsides of the dough up and over the outer edge of the vegetables so some vegetables are tucked under the crust. Pinch together any gaps in the dough. The shape will be free-form and does not need to be perfect—that's the beauty of it.

For the coating, brush the edges of the dough with egg and sprinkle the Parmesan all over the filling and crust. Bake for 22 to 25 minutes. The galette should be a nice golden-brown color on top.

Let the galette cool for 10 minutes. Slice and serve with a drizzle of the remaining sauce on top.

NOTE

You can double this recipe and make an extra galette that you can freeze for up to a month. To reheat, simply take the extra galette out of the freezer and place it on a baking sheet. Bake in the oven at 350°F for about 25 minutes. You won't have the extra sauce on hand, but that's easy to whip up (or it's delicious even without it).

honey dijon salmon

MAKES 4 SERVINGS   PREP TIME: 10 minutes   COOK TIME: 10 minutes

¼ cup honey

¼ cup Dijon mustard

Four 5-ounce salmon fillets

Salt and freshly ground
black pepper

2 tablespoons unsalted butter

twin tip

Dijon mustard is different from
standard yellow mustard because
it contains ground-up mustard
seeds (not just mustard powder)
and a little bit of white wine,
along with some extra spices.
Dijon mustard typically is a tan
color, not bright yellow like regular
mustard, which has turmeric
added to enhance its color. Dijon
has a tangier and more complex
flavor than regular mustard, which
is why it's our go-to for recipes
like this.

This is one of our mom's favorite dishes. It's super-easy, it's fast,
and it has just a few simple ingredients. It's great for a weeknight
meal, or fancy enough to serve if you have people over. Enjoy it
with some rice or maybe quickly sautéed green beans.

Sometimes your store will have salmon with the skin on. If you
don't like the skin, cook it with the salmon anyway, because it
adds flavor. You can easily remove it when you serve the fish.

In a bowl, mix the honey and Dijon mustard together to make a
sauce.

Lay the salmon on a plate and prick each side of it with a fork.

Season each side of the salmon with salt and pepper. Heavily
baste one side of each piece with the honey Dijon sauce, so it
drizzles down the side, reserving half of the sauce.

Heat a frying pan over medium-high heat and add the butter to
the pan. When the butter has melted, place the salmon in the pan,
basted-side down. As the salmon cooks, baste the other side with
the sauce.

Cook for 4 to 5 minutes on each side and carefully flip with a spatula. (Resist the urge to flip before 4 minutes, because you want the
sauce to caramelize so each side of the salmon becomes a beautiful
golden brown.) Transfer to a plate and serve.

taking fab food photos

If you look at any one of our family's phones, you'll see a million food pictures. We try not to let a good food moment pass if it's picture-worthy.

Our house and kitchen are hilarious at mealtimes. We'll make a meal, but we won't sit down and eat it like a normal family. Instead, we'll plate one dish nice and pretty, pull in the portable lights we keep next to the kitchen, set up some accessories to add color, texture, and dimension, and then take a ton of photos. This can be hard for the person whose plate is the star, because eating has to wait until the photo session is done!

We're now pretty decent at taking a good photo. We used to be horrible, and if you look back at our old Instagram photos, they're all dark and not very appetizing. From experience, trial and error, and watching tutorials about photographing food, we've learned a lot about lighting and styling.

If you're just getting into food photography yourself, here are some of the best tricks we can share.

Go outside. If you have an outdoor space where you can take a photo, that's your best environment for lighting and color. Use what you have in nature and outdoor accessories to accent your photo. For instance:

- Hold a plate or bowl above grass or flowers for a vibrant natural backsplash.

- Set the dish on an outdoor table or on the patio stones for an earthy look.

- Bring the outdoors in—maybe a few blades of grass, some ferns or flowers, fall foliage, pinecones, or even an icicle to stylize seasonally.

Think about the best way to photograph your food. Sometimes, that means taking a single photo of the ingredients. Other times, you may want to take a series of photos to show how something is chopped, how it looks as it sautés, and how it looks when it's done.

Stage lights are a great investment if you can afford them, because they really brighten up the photo setting. (When we use them, one of us holds the light directly over the food shot and the other takes the photo.)

Pay attention to little details. For instance, add garnishes on or around your plates. A sprig of parsley, cherry tomatoes, a sprinkling of almonds or chocolate chips, or flower petals from your yard can make a great color accent.

Put your food on a plate or bowl that complements it well. If you need more color, add a bright napkin or some table linens into the mix. If you don't use a tablecloth, pick a surface (wooden table, marble countertop) that works well with the dish. You want a variety of colors and patterns, along with textures and angles that accentuate the dish's best features.

Stand on a chair, put your photo props on the table, and photograph right on top of your subject.

Tweak if needed. You probably won't need to do a lot of editing, but sometimes brightening the photo or adding a small amount of contrast can make it "pop."

Shop thrift stores for unique dishes or table linens, or ask people to give them to you as gifts. Our family always gifts us fun new plates, bowls, napkins, and other stuff to use in our food shots. We're probably easy to shop for, as our photo shoots are never-ending and we love these kinds of presents!

creamy polenta with eggs and bacon

MAKES 5 SERVINGS   PREP TIME: 15 minutes   COOK TIME: 30 minutes

POLENTA

3½ cups water

3 cups vegetable or chicken broth

1 cup yellow cornmeal (stone ground)

2 tablespoons extra-virgin olive oil

¼ cup milk

TOPPING

6 slices well-done bacon, crumbled (or Fakin' Bacon, cooked and crumbled, see Notes)

5 eggs (1 egg per person)

1 cup shredded cheese (choose your favorite; we like freshly grated Parmesan or sharp Cheddar)

⅓ cup finely chopped fresh Italian parsley

Extra-virgin olive oil for drizzling

Salt and freshly ground black pepper

Polenta and grits look a lot alike, but polenta is made from a finer and smoother cornmeal. Our dish is kind of like cheesy grits, but it's creamier—especially with a perfectly fried egg on top, which we pop so the yolk can serve as the "gravy." We like to serve this with a simple arugula and tomato salad. The polenta is rich, and a light salad is a refreshing complement.

This is a really filling meal. We nearly always go for "seconds" in our house, but with this dish we're all satisfied after one serving.

One note: This recipe requires a lot of stirring, so you might want to share this job with someone else. (Luckily, we have each other!) If you can't take turns with a buddy, just put on some good music, stir to the rhythm, and have fun.

To make the polenta, bring the water and broth to a boil in a heavy pot (preferably nonstick). Turn the heat to medium and, using a wooden spoon, slowly stir in the cornmeal and bring back to a simmer, stirring slowly and continuously.

When you've added all the cornmeal, turn the heat down to low and continue to stir slowly. The key here is to avoid letting the polenta get lumpy. Continue to stir for 20 to 25 minutes, until the polenta is thick and pulling away from the sides of the pot. (Check the directions on your polenta package, as the cooking time may vary slightly from brand to brand.)

When the polenta is done, stir in the olive oil and milk. Cover and set aside.

To make the topping, in the same pan that you cooked your bacon in, cook your eggs so they are lightly fried (about 1 minute on each side). Don't overcook your eggs, because then you will have less yolk "gravy."

To serve, divide the polenta among five bowls, then add the toppings to each bowl: a generous serving of the cheese, a fried egg, some bacon bits, a sprinkle of parsley, a nice drizzle of olive oil, and salt and pepper to taste.

Now if you are Lyla, you will ruin this pretty plate quickly by pushing everything all together!

NOTES

If you're a vegetarian, try substituting Fakin' Bacon for the bacon in this recipe. This is a smoked tempeh product you can find in the natural food sections of many grocery stores. We've also found vegetarian bacon bits that are good.

Polenta firms up quickly, so you can always stir in a little more liquid to make it creamy again.

twin tips

Wash your herbs well. Often, in addition to rinsing fresh herbs, we soak them and shake them in a bowl of water and check the bottom of the bowl for dirt or sand granules. If we find any, we rinse or soak the herbs again until we're sure they're clean.

If you have leftover herbs, roll them up in a paper or cotton towel and store them in the fridge.

make-your-own wild rice bowls

MAKES 4 TO 5 SERVINGS

PREP TIME: 20 minutes   COOK TIME: 40 minutes (or time specified on your package of rice)

RICE AND VEGGIES

2 cups dry wild rice

2 ears of corn, cooked and kernels cut off, or 1 cup frozen, thawed corn

1 cup diced tomatoes (cherry tomatoes are the sweetest)

1 cup peeled and diced cucumber (about 1 cucumber)

2 avocados, peeled and diced

1 cup crumbled feta cheese

1 can mandarin orange segments, drained

1 cup sliced almonds

DRESSING

⅓ cup packed finely chopped fresh Italian parsley

½ cup extra-virgin olive oil

2 teaspoons honey

2 tablespoons white wine vinegar

¼ teaspoon salt

A few cranks of black pepper

twin tip

When we have leftover rice, we save it and use it later to make super-quick fried rice: heat a little oil in a saucepan and add the leftover rice, any frozen veggies you have on hand, and a couple tablespoons of broth or water. Drizzle on a touch of soy sauce, scramble an egg into the rice, and sauté everything until it's heated through and the egg cooks and coats the rice and veggies.

Are you always tinkering with your dishes to satisfy people who ask, "Can you leave the mushrooms out?" or "Can I have some extra avocado?" With a buffet-style topping bar like this, your guests can tailor-make their meals, so everyone is happy.

Also, this makes a really quick weeknight meal. You can make the dressing and cook the rice 2 days ahead of time.

We've used our favorite mix of ingredients here, but you can add anything you want to this recipe to make it your own (see options, below).

To make the rice and veggies, cook the rice according to the package directions. We usually serve it at room temperature or just a bit warm.

Place the corn, tomatoes, cucumber, avocado, feta, mandarin oranges, and almonds in their own bowls with serving utensils.

To make the dressing, place the parsley, olive oil, honey, vinegar, salt, and pepper in a blender. Blend well, until the parsley is just speckles, and then transfer to an easy-to-pour jar. (You can also put this in a jar and use an immersion blender.)

Place the rice, dressing, and all other ingredients on the table so your guests can make their own rice-veggie bowl with their preferred ingredients.

INGREDIENT OPTIONS

Broccoli, steamed	Rotisserie chicken, shredded
Carrots, shredded or chopped	Sausage, cooked and sliced
Cheddar cheese, shredded	Shrimp, cooked
Chickpeas	Sunflower seeds
Edamame	Walnuts
Grapes, sliced	

cheesy rice cakes

MAKES APPROXIMATELY 20 RICE CAKES (4 SERVINGS)
PREP TIME: 25 minutes (includes time to cook the rice)   COOK TIME: 20 minutes

1 cup dry Jasmati or basmati rice (will make about 3 cups cooked rice)

½ cup finely chopped fresh Italian parsley

½ cup finely chopped fresh dill

½ cup grated Parmesan cheese

¾ cup shredded sharp Cheddar cheese

½ teaspoon salt

⅛ teaspoon freshly ground black pepper

1 teaspoon cornstarch

2 large eggs, beaten

Unsalted butter for cooking the cakes

Applesauce, store-bought or homemade (page 26), or crème fraîche

These rice cakes have a great griddle flavor and nice crunch on the outside, and they are packed with herbs and cheese. We eat them like finger food, dunking them into applesauce or crème fraîche.

If you haven't tried crème fraîche yet, you definitely should. It's a little like sour cream, but it's richer, thicker, and less tangy. It's indulgently delicious, and it will highlight the flavor of anything you eat.

Preheat the oven to 200°F. Line a baking sheet with parchment paper. Cook the rice according to the package directions, letting it sit for 10 minutes after removing it from the heat.

Pour the warm rice into a large mixing bowl and add the parsley, dill, Parmesan cheese, Cheddar cheese, salt, pepper, cornstarch, and eggs. Blend until all the ingredients are incorporated.

Heat a cast-iron or nonstick skillet over medium heat and add 1 to 2 teaspoons of butter to cover the bottom of the pan. Using a tablespoon, scoop rounded dollops of the rice, place them in the pan, and gently flatten them with a spatula sprayed with cooking spray (to keep the cakes from sticking to it). Let them crisp up on one side for about 4 minutes, then flip and cook for another 4 minutes, then transfer to the baking sheet and place in the oven to keep warm while you cook the remaining rice cakes. Add another 1 to 2 teaspoons of butter to the skillet between batches.

Serve the rice cakes with applesauce or crème fraîche.

Don't overcrowd your pan, because then it's hard to flip your food. This is a good general rule we learned from the judges on *Chopped Junior*, because one of us (we won't tell you who) crowded the pan in the entrée round, and the dish didn't cook well.

A cast-iron pan gives a nice crispiness to the cakes. We got ours as a gift from our parents; you can find one at Amazon or a store like Home Goods. Just follow the directions on how to care for your pan, because you'll ruin it if you wash it the regular way.

twin tip

Always use a plastic or silicone spatula on nonstick surfaces. That way, you won't scratch the pan.

golden black beans

1 sweet onion, diced

2 tablespoons extra-virgin olive oil

Two 15-ounce cans black beans, drained and rinsed

One 13- to 14-ounce can full-fat coconut milk (shake the can well before opening)

1 cup frozen corn

1 teaspoon ground turmeric

1 teaspoon ground cumin

½ teaspoon salt

2 cups cooked rice or quinoa (optional)

Diced radish, chopped cilantro, and/or diced avocado for garnish

twin tip

Turmeric stains like crazy. To avoid creating laundry problems, don't wear white when you're eating foods that contain turmeric, and don't wipe your hands on white dish towels without rinsing your hands first. If you do get turmeric on a counter, it will come up with Bartender's Friend soft cleanser.

When we were little, our mom called black beans "chocolate beans" to make us like them more. It worked, and now we're hooked on them. We call this dish Golden Black Beans because the turmeric turns the broth golden.

This is what's called a one-pot meal, which makes it perfect for a quick weeknight dinner. You can serve it as is, which is kind of thick and soupy, or you can serve it over rice (making it two pots).

By the way, ask five people how to pronounce turmeric, and we swear everyone will say it a different way. Is it *too-maric* or *tur-mer-ick*? We switch it up and just wait for people to correct us.

In a medium saucepan, sauté the onion in the olive oil over medium heat for 8 to 10 minutes, until it's transparent and getting a touch golden brown.

Add the beans, coconut milk, corn, turmeric, cumin, and salt. Cook for about 10 more minutes. Serve in a bowl alone or over rice. Garnish with some radish, cilantro, and avocado. Add salt to taste and serve.

NOTES

Eat this if you feel a cold coming on, because turmeric is really good for you and research shows that it wards off infections.

This broth is not meant to cook down. It's meant to be soupy and satisfying, and to make a nice gravy if you serve this over rice.

mediterranean stuffed peppers

MAKES 6 TO 8 STUFFED PEPPERS   PREP TIME: 25 minutes   COOK TIME: 30 minutes

1 cup dry golden couscous (you can use gluten-free couscous if desired)

2 tablespoons unsalted butter

One 19.6-ounce jar long-stem, oil-marinated artichoke hearts (don't drain these)

¼ cup packed finely chopped fresh Italian parsley

1 cup crumbled feta cheese

2 tablespoons capers, drained

½ cup oil-marinated sun-dried tomatoes, drained and finely chopped

6 to 8 medium yellow, red, or orange bell peppers, or a combination, tops cut off and seeds removed

twin tip

Kitchen scissors rock, because you can use them to cut food (like the artichokes in this recipe) right over the bowl. We also cut food into pieces in the bowl itself, pointing the scissors downward. They're great for snipping herbs, too.

This is a flavorful crowd-pleaser, and it's super-simple because couscous is ready in a snap.

We usually buy the big packs of multicolored red, yellow, and orange peppers. These make the dish even prettier. We like to use Cento brand Roman artichokes because the artichokes are packed in the seasoned oil that's needed for this recipe, and the jar is just the right size. However, any brand of artichokes packed in seasoned oil will do.

Preheat the oven to 425°F.

Cook the couscous according to the directions on the package, adding the butter to the water.

Chop the artichokes into ¼-inch pieces and place them in a large mixing bowl. Add ½ cup of the oil from the artichoke jar to the bowl. Add the parsley, feta, capers, and sun-dried tomatoes to the bowl, further chopping them if you need to. Add the couscous and mix the ingredients well.

Stuff the peppers to the top with the couscous mixture, mounding it so there's a small dome on top. Place the peppers in a large baking pan that has sides tall enough to hold the peppers upright. Bake for 30 minutes. If you have leftovers, these are as good cold as they are hot.

NOTE

When you use up your sun-dried tomatoes, keep the oil. You can use it as a bread dipping sauce or sauté eggs or veggies in it.

cauliflower truffle lasagna

MAKES 6 TO 8 SERVINGS   PREP TIME: 30 minutes   COOK TIME: 1 hour

1 medium-large cauliflower head

¼ cup extra-virgin olive oil

2 shallot bulbs, diced
(about ¼ cup)

1 teaspoon salt

¼ teaspoon freshly ground
black pepper

1¼ cups whole milk

¼ cup vegetable broth

¼ cup grated Parmesan cheese

½ teaspoon ground nutmeg

2 tablespoons truffle oil, plus
more for serving

⅔ cup chopped fresh Italian
parsley

1½ cups shredded sharp
Cheddar cheese

1 cup shredded mozzarella

One 9-ounce box no-boil
lasagna noodles (you won't need
the whole box unless you double
the recipe)

We have a large family—aunts, uncles, cousins, grandparents—and everyone has very personal food preferences. If people don't want to try something we cook, we (usually) aren't offended, although we'll pester them to taste it because we see it as a challenge.

We usually can get people to try a new recipe, and most of the time they like it. However, we know that some people will never be convinced. But when we make this lasagna, everyone likes it, and they are SO surprised—especially because there's no meat in it, and our extended family enjoys meat with main meals.

Whether you like cauliflower or not, we urge you to try this recipe. We think you will become a big fan of cauliflower cooked this way, and we also think you will agree that truffle oil has one of the best flavors and aromas in the world.

Preheat the oven to 350°F and grease a 9 by 13-inch baking pan.

Remove the outer leaves of the cauliflower and cut the base stem so it is flush with the crown. Then chop the cauliflower florets and stems into ½-inch pieces. (It's fine if it gets all crumbly; you'll add the crumbly bits to the pan as well.)

In a large sauté pan, heat the olive oil over medium heat and add the shallots. Sauté the shallots for 1 to 2 minutes, until they are transparent. Add the cauliflower, salt, and pepper and sauté, stirring occasionally, for about 10 minutes.

→

Add the milk and veggie broth, cover, and cook for about 10 minutes longer, or until the cauliflower is just softened. Transfer the mixture to a food processor or blender. Add the Parmesan cheese, nutmeg, and truffle oil, and blend until pureed.

In a separate bowl, mix the chopped parsley, Cheddar cheese, and mozzarella.

Now it's time to assemble the lasagna: Spread approximately ½ cup of the cauliflower puree in the bottom of the pan (enough so the bottom is just covered with the puree). Add a layer of lasagna noodles (we end up breaking some of the noodles to fill in gaps). Add 1½ cups cauliflower puree, distributing it evenly and covering all of the edges of the noodles. Add half of the cheese mixture, distributing it evenly. Add a layer of lasagna noodles. Add the rest of the cauliflower puree, making sure all of the noodles are covered (if the noodles aren't covered with puree, they will get crunchy when baked). Sprinkle the remaining cheese mixture evenly over the top. Cover loosely with foil (be sure to tent it to avoid getting cheese stuck to the foil) and bake for 40 minutes. Remove and let cool for about 10 minutes before cutting and serving. After plating each piece, drizzle it with about ¼ teaspoon of truffle oil.

NOTES

You'll find truffle oil in the grocery store, and a little goes a long way. A small bottle will give you plenty to make this lasagna.

If you'd like to use whole nutmeg, which is what we do, you can grind it easily on the small holes on a box grater. Always grind more than you need and store the extra in a baggie or jar.

If you want a little meat, you can sprinkle pancetta or bacon on top of the cooked lasagna.

smothered vegetable primavera

PASTA

1 tablespoon salt

One 1-pound box pasta
(farfalle or penne)

SAUCE

5 tablespoons extra-virgin
olive oil

2 sweet onions, diced into
¼-inch pieces

3 cups broccoli florets, diced into
¼-inch pieces

2 red, yellow, or orange bell
peppers, or a combination, tops
removed, seeded, and diced into
¼-inch pieces

20 mini cherry tomatoes, halved

1 teaspoon salt, plus more to taste

¼ teaspoon freshly ground black
pepper, plus more to taste

2 medium garlic cloves, minced

½ cup grated Parmesan cheese,
plus more for serving

¼ cup chopped basil

twin tip

The water in which you cook your
pasta contains starch, so it helps
make the sauce silkier.

Whatever pasta you pick for this recipe is fine (although we like farfalle or penne best). What really matters here is cooking the veggies down to make a creamy, smothered veggie primavera dish. One key here is to make sure your veggies are cut into small pieces.

To make the pasta, fill a large stockpot two-thirds full with water and bring to a boil over high heat. Just before adding the pasta, add the salt to the water.

Cook the pasta according to the instructions on the box. Very important: Before you strain the pasta, ladle out 1 cup of the pasta water and set it aside.

To make the sauce, place a large sauté pan over medium heat and add 3 tablespoons of the olive oil. Add the onions and cook, stirring occasionally, until they are transparent and light brown (8 to 10 minutes).

Add the broccoli, peppers, tomatoes, ½ teaspoon of the salt, the pepper, and the remaining 2 tablespoons olive oil, and let the mixture cook down for 15 to 20 minutes, stirring occasionally. Your vegetables should all be cooked through and softened. Turn the heat to low and add the minced garlic. Cook for another 5 minutes, stirring occasionally.

Remove the veggies from the heat and add the cooked and strained pasta to the sauté pan. Toss the pasta with the veggies and then stir in ¼ cup or more of the reserved pasta water, depending on the consistency you like (see Twin Tip). Add the Parmesan and basil and toss. Season with additional salt, pepper, and Parmesan and serve.

artichokes with lemony dip

LEMONY DIP

¼ cup plus 1 tablespoon sliced
or slivered almonds

½ cup extra-virgin olive oil

¼ teaspoon salt

Zest and juice of 1 lemon
(see Notes)

1 small garlic clove, minced

2 tablespoons mayonnaise

4 to 6 artichokes

We like to make these artichokes the center of a meal, serving them with a good bread, half an avocado, and hard-boiled eggs. (We make this look fancy by putting the sliced eggs in the cavities of the avocados.) The result looks very French and sophisticated, and it's perfect to photograph. As we eat this meal, we always end up dunking our bread and any veggies into the tangy lemon sauce.

By the way, the first time we tried steamed artichokes was at a restaurant called Main Street in Princeton, New Jersey. We always went there for Mother's Day with our mom, aunt, and grandmother. We made a habit of ordering their artichokes, because it was an event to eat one. One of our special memories is the time our mom took just the two of us to Main Street on a late afternoon on Christmas Eve and ordered artichokes as a special treat for us to enjoy before the evening festivities.

The last time we ate at Main Street for Mother's Day, they no longer had the artichokes on their menu. We are sad to say that they closed soon after that. Coincidence? Maybe not.

To make the dip, put the almonds, olive oil, salt, lemon zest and juice, garlic, and mayonnaise in a blender and blend until smooth. (If your sauce separates before serving, just give it a good mix with a fork.)

To prepare the artichokes, wash them and cut off the long stem so there's just about ½ to 1 inch of stem left. Using a serrated knife, saw off the domed part of the artichoke, leaving a flat head. It's hard to cut the top off, but while this is optional, it's a good idea because it lets more of the steam into the artichoke to soften the leaves. You can also pull off some of the outermost leaves, as these won't provide much meat.

Fill a large stockpot with about 3 inches of water, cover, and bring to a simmer. Put the artichokes stem-side up in a steamer basket, place the steamer basket in the pot, and cover. (They seem to steam better stem-side up. We've tested this.)

Set over medium-low heat and simmer-steam for 30 minutes, depending on the size of your artichokes. (Watch the water—we steamed ours too long one time and all the water ran out, which could have been dangerous.) Add more water if you need to.

The artichokes are ready when you can easily insert a knife in the stem, the leaves pull off easily, and the meat at the base of the leaf is tender. Make sure you test this. You can serve the artichokes hot, at room temperature, or chilled.

NOTES

"Zesting" means scraping tiny pieces off the peel of a citrus fruit using either a zester or the side of a box grater that has very small pinprick-size holes.

Wash the lemon and dry it before zesting it. Zest before you juice the lemon; otherwise, it'll be very hard to zest it because you can't grip it easily.

Avoid zesting the white part of a lemon or any other citrus fruit, because it's bitter.

twin tip

If you haven't tried eating an artichoke before, here's how you eat the leaves. Simply pull off a leaf, dunk the stem side of the leaf in the sauce, and then put it in your mouth and pull, using your teeth to scrape off the meat on the bottom third of the leaf. That's it.

Once you have stripped and eaten all of the leaf meat, pull out the rest of the leaves. With a sharp knife, cut out the furlike stuff at an angle (you can also scrape it off with a spoon) so you can reach the heart. Cut the heart into quarters and enjoy. (Our mom usually ends up in charge of prepping all the artichoke hearts, including our dad's. She's had more than forty years of practice doing this, so we trust that she'll keep this treasure intact.)

desserts

When we're craving something sweet, we frequently go simple. For instance, we'll make our garden-fresh version of Sour Patch Kids: a stevia leaf and a lemon sorrel leaf rolled up together. (It's a garden treat we were introduced to at our school's orientation.) Other favorite treats around our house include whole dates and frozen sliced bananas, which taste just like candy.

Of course, we also love to get in the kitchen and bake—especially around the holidays. One of our earliest memories is coming downstairs in the morning to find the wonderful aroma of fresh-baked Christmas cookies greeting us. We hopped right in the kitchen and helped make the second batch (while we wolfed down the first batch).

Whether you're in the mood for simple or fancy, we've got you covered here. You'll find everything from Tropical Baked Custard (page 143) to The Ultimate Peanut Butter Cookies (page 161), along with a couple of killer shakes (pages 145 and 146).

deep dark chocolate pudding

⅛ teaspoon salt

½ cup plus 2 tablespoons sugar

⅓ cup unsweetened cocoa powder

3 tablespoons cornstarch

2¼ cups whole milk (no substitutions)

1 tablespoon unsalted butter

Toppings (see below)

twin tip

When you cook with cornstarch, always mix it into a cold or room-temperature liquid. If you mix it into a hot liquid, it'll get lumpy.

This pudding is pure, rich, chocolaty bliss. We eat it warm right off the stove in the winter, and chilled in the summer. Grab a small mug and a little spoon—because each bite has a huge amount of flavor—and prepare to have magic on your taste buds.

Our mom is an uber dark chocolate fan, and we have to hide this pudding from her. (We're not being devious; she told us to do it.)

In a large saucepan, mix together the salt, sugar, cocoa powder, and cornstarch. Turn the burner to medium heat and slowly stir in the milk, ¼ cup at a time. Cook for 6 to 7 minutes, until the mixture comes to a light simmer. Continue to simmer, whisking lightly, until the mixture starts to thicken and clings to the whisk. (This will take about 2 more minutes.)

Remove from the heat and stir in the butter until the butter is completely melted and the pudding is well mixed. Enjoy warm right away or pour the mixture into a non-plastic container with a lid and put it in the fridge to cool for an hour. The pudding is best served the same day. When you take this out of the fridge, stir it up really well. The cornstarch makes it Jellolike, and a good stir turns it back into pudding. For added flair, put on any of the toppings below.

TOPPING OPTIONS

Biscotti

Chopped pecans

Grated cinnamon

Mint leaves

Orange zest

Raspberries

Toasted shredded coconut

Whipped cream

fruit fritters

1 cup oat flour (see Twin Tip) or unbleached all-purpose flour

2 teaspoons baking powder

1 teaspoon ground cinnamon

2 tablespoons granulated sugar

1 egg, beaten

½ cup canned full-fat coconut milk (shake the can well before opening)

1 ripe banana, diced

5 large (or 10 small) strawberries, hulled and diced

1½ cups vegetable oil for frying

Cinnamon sugar, confectioners' sugar, or a dollop of Greek yogurt with a teaspoon of honey drizzled over it for topping (optional)

twin tip

We make our own oat flour with old-fashioned rolled oats (not instant oats). We use our Vitamix to blend the oats until they're very fine. If you try this yourself, don't overload your blender. Just blend a little at a time; otherwise, you won't get a flourlike texture.

These fruit fritters are GOOD, and perfect for any occasion. We serve them with a sprinkling of cinnamon sugar or confectioners' sugar or a dollop of honey and yogurt. The fruit inside the fritters gets warm and soft, and makes a nice complement to the rich batter.

In a medium bowl, mix the flour, baking powder, cinnamon, and granulated sugar. Add the egg and coconut milk and mix well. The batter will be thick.

Add the diced banana and strawberries and stir so the fruit is evenly distributed.

Put the oil in a large stockpot (using a large pot will reduce splattering) and heat it for about 4 minutes over medium heat. To cook, carefully add tablespoon-size portions of the fritter mix to the oil. (We use a cookie scooper.) The oil should be sizzling hot when you add the fritter batter in.

Let the fritters brown for about 2 minutes. Use a slotted spoon to flip them and cook them for an additional 2 minutes. As the fritters cook, they'll turn a very dark, rich brown; you want the batter to be cooked through.

Carefully remove the fritters from the oil and place them on a paper towel-lined plate. Serve with desired toppings.

tropical baked custard

2 ripe bananas, sliced

3 large eggs

One 13- to 14-ounce can full-fat coconut milk (shake the can well before opening)

1 cup pineapple juice

3 tablespoons granulated sugar

¾ cup unbleached all-purpose flour

Pinch of salt

Confectioners' sugar, finely diced banana or pineapple, or vanilla ice cream for topping (optional)

We probably should own a coconut grove, because we're always using canned coconut milk in our recipes. It's the number one ingredient we keep in stock, and if Costco ever stops selling it, we don't know what we'll do!

In case you're wondering, coconut milk doesn't actually add a coconut flavor to foods. Instead, it helps create the perfect texture, acting like butter and heavy cream in one.

In this incredibly light dessert, the coconut milk acts as a supporting player for the bananas and pineapple. The result will wow your taste buds with a flavor that takes you somewhere warm and tropical.

Preheat the oven to 400°F. Thoroughly grease the bottom and sides of an 8 by 11-inch ovenproof casserole dish. (You can also use a 10-inch cast-iron skillet or Dutch oven.)

Place the sliced bananas in a single layer in the bottom of the dish.

In a bowl, beat the eggs. Add the coconut milk, pineapple juice, 2 tablespoons of the granulated sugar, the flour, and the salt. Mix well.

Pour into the casserole dish and sprinkle the remaining 1 tablespoon of granulated sugar on top. Bake for 45 to 50 minutes, until the custard is "set," meaning solid.

Let cool for 15 minutes and then serve with desired toppings, or store in the fridge to eat later. The custard will keep in the fridge for up to 2 days.

maple milkshake

¼ cup maple syrup

2½ frozen ripe bananas

1 cup milk

½ cup canned full-fat coconut milk (shake the can well before opening)

twin tip

Don't throw away brown bananas. Instead, peel them and store them in the freezer in a zip-top bag or plastic container for 3 to 4 months. You'll want to keep a stash, because this recipe will become a regular!

Sometimes when we're craving a milkshake, we don't have ice cream in the freezer. But you know us by now, so you know what we do: We reach for a can of coconut milk. It makes this shake every bit as rich and creamy as the traditional milkshake made with ice cream.

We're so crazy about this milkshake that we typically drink the first batch, make a second batch, and then stick our fingers (safely) in the unplugged blender to lick up the rest. Seriously, it *rocks*. Our dad, who's the picky one in the family, ranks it as his favorite shake, beating out his previous favorite chocolate shake. He's almost fifty years young, and he's tasted a lot of milkshakes, so we think that's a true compliment.

Add the maple syrup, bananas, milk, and coconut milk to a blender and blend on high speed until smooth and creamy.

mocha milkshake

1½ cups vanilla ice cream

½ cup prepared coffee (decaf or regular)

½ cup canned full-fat coconut milk (shake the can well before opening)

2 tablespoons unsweetened cocoa powder

twin tip

Rather than brewing and chilling coffee for this recipe, we usually just pour leftover coffee from our parents' coffee pot into a jar and save it in the fridge. But they drink high-voltage regular coffee (as our mom calls it), so if we're serving this milkshake close to bedtime, we use decaf coffee instead.

We love coffee, vanilla ice cream, chocolate, and coconut milk, so this is taste-bud heaven for us. It's rich, so while it's not "supersized," your sweet tooth will feel super-satisfied.

Sometimes we eat this slowly with a spoon so we can really enjoy it. Other times, we chug it down fast. Either way works!

Add the ice cream, coffee, coconut milk, and cocoa to a blender. Blend until the shake is smooth and creamy.

inventing your own recipes

People often ask us how we get the ideas for recipes. We don't really have any set system, but a variety of things can inspire us:

ONE: We're hungry!

We look in the fridge and cabinets, check out the fruit and vegetable bowls, and see a variety of raw ingredients. So we say, "Hmmmm. What can we make with a can of white beans, baby tomatoes, garlic, lemon, and olive oil?"

And boom: We immediately think that we can take these ingredients in two or three different directions. So what do we want—a snack, a main meal, or a sauce?

A snack would mean a dip like roasted tomato white bean dip. We slow-roast the tomatoes and then blend them with the white beans, garlic, lemon, and olive oil. Delish with veggies or tortilla chips.

A main meal would mean we'd sauté the garlic, white beans, and tomatoes together, add in some broth or milk and lemon, and wind up with a stewy-type dish. Yum.

A sauce would probably mean we throw all of this in a blender with some milk or broth or something and serve it on top of rice, pasta, or quinoa. Hearty goodness.

This process is usually pretty simple and quick—because we're hungry and need to eat!—so it's easy to recall and write down the ingredients. Later, if we make our creation a couple more times and like the results, we'll formalize it into a recipe.

TWO: We're bored and need something to do

In this case, we start with the creative question, "I wonder what will happen if I mix these ingredients, bake it this way, and serve it that way?" There are no guarantees that our explorations will deliver an awesome recipe, and our experiments can be messy and even wasteful. We're grateful that our parents are patient, because our mom hates waste—along with sticky refrigerator door handles, floury drawer knobs, and splattered stove tops!

As we've grown as cooks, we've gotten to know ingredients better and respect the science of cooking, so our creations have become more successful. Some of our pairings—for instance, peas and pears, maple syrup and corn, and potatoes and applesauce—may seem a little weird, but we've discovered through experimentation that they're complementary.

If a recipe doesn't work the first time but we like the general taste, then we'll persist and figure out how to make it work, reworking it and cooking it a new way. This is how we invented our Tropical Baked Custard (page 143). The recipe started out as tropical crepes, but they were really a pain to make and fell apart. The taste was fantastic, however, so we reworked the recipe into a custard—it turned out to be insanely good.

THREE: Something inspired us

Sometimes we'll get our hands on a new ingredient, see an interesting recipe or technique on a cooking show, or decide to try a new twist on something we ate at a restaurant.

For instance, we knew we loved artichokes because we had them at a restaurant. However, we wanted a lemon dip that stuck to an artichoke leaf rather than drippy butter. The result: our Artichokes with Lemony Dip on page 134.

Similarly, our love of flourless chocolate cake inspired us to try making a strawberry flourless cake. It was a disaster, but we kept trying, and our experiments finally led us down the path to our Fruit Fritters on page 142—pretty different results, but it was all part of the process. And we wound up with the taste we were aiming for.

mint chocolate cookie brittle

PREP TIME: 25 minutes   COOK TIME: 15 minutes   FREEZER TIME: 20 minutes

COOKIE BRITTLE

½ cup unsalted butter, softened

½ cup sugar

1 egg

¾ teaspoon peppermint extract

½ cup unsweetened cocoa powder

¾ cup oat flour (see Twin Tip, page 142)

¼ teaspoon salt

½ teaspoon baking soda

CHOCOLATE ICING

One 10-ounce bag semisweet chocolate chips, or approximately 1½ cups (we like Ghirardelli because it melts well)

1½ teaspoons peppermint extract

We've gone back and forth when it comes to eating gluten. Generally, we try not to eat a ton of it.

When Lyla first tried a gluten-free diet, we were Girl Scouts. As you can imagine, being a Girl Scout and not being able to eat Thin Mint cookies wasn't fun. All anyone talks about during cookie-selling season is Thin Mints, and our dad would basically eat a whole sleeve of them at a time.

Well, we took matters into our own hands and came up with what we think is an even better mint-chocolate combination. As you may remember from chapter 1, Lyla accidentally dropped a tray of these once, and because they were brittle, they broke into pieces. This mistake worked for us, because we discovered that cookie brittle is lots of fun to eat.

Preheat the oven to 350°F.

To make the brittle, using a stand or hand mixer, cream the butter and sugar together until they reach a creamy, even consistency. Add the egg and peppermint extract and blend until combined.

In a separate bowl, mix the cocoa powder, oat flour, salt, and baking soda. Add to the wet mixture and mix until the ingredients are fully blended.

Put the dough between 2 pieces of parchment paper and roll out until it is "cookie thin," about ¼ inch thick.

Remove the top layer of parchment and transfer the dough using the bottom layer of parchment to a baking sheet. Bake for 15 minutes. Remove from the oven and let cool for 10 minutes. These will crisp up while they cool. After the cookies are cool, make the icing.

To make the icing, melt the chocolate chips in a double boiler (see page 153). Once the chips are melted, thoroughly stir in the peppermint extract.

Pour the melted chocolate on top of the baked and cooled cookie. Using a rubber spatula, spread it out to cover the cookie layer completely.

Put the baking sheet in the freezer for about 20 minutes to let the chocolate harden. Break into cookie-size brittle pieces and eat! Store any leftovers in an airtight container in the fridge for up to 1 week. They stay crisper this way.

NOTES

Make sure you use peppermint extract, not spearmint.

When rolling your dough, you can use a rolling pin, a bottle, or whatever is handy. We frequently grab a bottle because our rolling pin is in the basement, and we get lazy. Basically, any sturdy, smallish cylinder works.

Peppermint extract has a very strong flavor. Don't measure it out directly over your bowl, because you may pour out too much and spill some of it. You definitely don't want to do that with this ingredient.

chocolate caramel pecan bark

MAKES 6 TO 8 SERVINGS

PREP TIME: 5 minutes   COOK TIME: 5 minutes   FREEZER TIME: 40 minutes

1 cup semisweet chocolate chips

¼ cup caramel sauce

⅓ cup pecan pieces

⅛ rounded teaspoon flaked sea salt

This bark makes a really nice gift at the holidays. We pack several pieces of the bark in a clear baggie, put the baggie inside a Chinese take-out carton, and add a ribbon.

Heat water in the bottom pot of a double boiler over medium-high heat (see Notes). Add the chocolate chips to the top part of the double boiler and stir frequently, until smooth and creamy. This should take about 5 minutes.

Line a baking sheet with parchment paper, pour the chocolate onto the sheet, and spread the chocolate out until it's about a ¼ inch thick. Drizzle the caramel onto the chocolate. Using a knife, cut through the caramel and chocolate to distribute the caramel flavor throughout. Evenly sprinkle the pecan pieces and sea salt onto the chocolate.

Freeze for 30 to 40 minutes and then break into pieces using your hands. You can store leftover bark in the fridge for a month.

NOTES

If you don't have a double boiler, put a couple inches of water in a large pot and heat over high heat until boiling. Turn the burner to low and rest a metal bowl on top of the pot (the bottom of the bowl should not touch the water). Add the chocolate to the bowl over the steaming water and stir until melted. Use oven mitts to hold the bowl, because it gets hot.

You can also melt chocolate chips in the microwave. Just put your chips in a microwave-safe bowl, microwave on 50 percent power for 1 minute, stir, and then microwave at 50 percent power for 20-second intervals until the chips melt. Be sure to stir after each interval, because the chips may be melted even if they still hold their shape.

mango rice pudding

¾ cup white basmati rice

Salt

2 cups water

⅓ cup plus 1 tablespoon sugar

2 tablespoons cornstarch

2¾ cups whole milk

1¼ cups fresh or frozen mango chunks, cut into small ¼-inch pieces (we use scissors to cut it up if it's frozen)

1 teaspoon vanilla extract

We are big fans of all types of rice dishes, so it's no surprise that we like rice for dessert, too!

Our neighbor Carol first introduced us to rice pudding. We took care of her cats at times and invited her over for holiday dinners with our family, and as a "thank you" she would bring us treats. One day she brought us rice pudding, and we fell in love with it. Our favorite version is this super-simple pudding, which has a delicious vanilla flavor accented with sweet, refreshing chunks of mango.

Our family would like to dedicate this recipe to Carol. She (along with our good friend Mrs. Terry) is the reason we're at the wonderful school we attend today, because they both encouraged us to apply. Carol was also a vegetarian and a huge animal lover—two more of our favorite things about her.

Combine the rice, ¼ teaspoon salt, and the water in a saucepan and bring to a boil over medium-high heat. (If you use a nonstick pan, it will make cleanup easier later.) Reduce the heat to a simmer, and cover and cook for 10 to 12 minutes, or until the liquid is absorbed. (Check to see if the rice needs to be rinsed and for the specific cooking time for your brand of rice, as it may be different.)

In a stockpot, combine the sugar and cornstarch and stir. Add the milk, mango, vanilla, and a pinch of salt. Turn the burner to medium-high heat and stir until everything is thoroughly mixed. Add the rice and bring to a low boil, reduce the heat, and cook at a low simmer for about 10 more minutes. Make sure your heat is low, because you don't want to scorch your milk.

Remove from the heat. Enjoy warm, or cool in the fridge for about an hour. Store in an airtight container in the fridge for up to 3 days.

NOTE

Fresh mango is wonderful, but it's a little easier to get a full cup's worth when you use frozen mango.

twin tips

The amount of fruit meat on a mango can be deceiving, because the pit takes up so much of the fruit. It's smart at first to buy more mangoes than you think you'll need.

A mango pit is really long and kind of flat, and you want to work with the pit—not against it. To cut the fruit meat off a mango, hold the mango vertically, resting it on a cutting board. With a knife, cut down on either side of the pit. (If you run into the pit, you will know.) Now, make long slits through each slab you've cut off (but not through the skin). Then flip the slab sort of "inside out" and scrape off the fruit.

gingerbread bread pudding

2 eggs

2½ cups milk

½ cup maple syrup

¾ teaspoon ground cinnamon

¼ teaspoon salt

1 apple, cored and diced into small pieces (keep the skin on)

¼ cup coconut oil, melted

6 cups of 1-inch-cubed gingerbread, store-bought or homemade (recipe follows)

This recipe makes us happy, because it makes our whole house smell like a gingerbread house.

We decided years ago that making a gingerbread house is fun but a little frustrating, because you can't eat the house. That's why we came up with a gingerbread recipe we could eat and share with friends.

This is actually two recipes in one, and it takes some time, but it is *so* worth it. This is one of the most delicious desserts you can make for holiday festivities, and it will fill your home with the aromas of ginger, cinnamon, and nutmeg—yum!

Preheat the oven to 350°F.

In a large bowl, mix the eggs, milk, maple syrup, cinnamon, salt, and apple. Slowly add the melted coconut oil.

Add the cubed gingerbread and gently stir to coat all of the bread pieces.

Pour the mixture into a greased, high-sided casserole dish (we use an 8½ by 11-inch casserole dish). Gently press down on the gingerbread so it's incorporated.

Bake for 45 minutes, or until the pudding part is set and not liquidy. Remove from the oven and let cool for 10 minutes before serving.

Gingerbread

MAKES 6 SERVINGS (enough gingerbread for 1 pudding plus extra to snack on)

PREP TIME: 15 minutes   COOK TIME: 40 minutes

¼ cup coconut oil, melted

½ cup molasses

½ cup plain Greek yogurt (2% or full-fat)

½ cup unsweetened, smooth applesauce, store-bought or homemade (page 26)

2 eggs

1 teaspoon vanilla extract

¼ cup packed light brown sugar

2 cups unbleached all-purpose flour (you can also make this with gluten-free flour)

½ teaspoon baking powder

1 teaspoon baking soda

¼ teaspoon salt

1½ teaspoons ground ginger

¼ teaspoon ground cloves

½ teaspoon ground nutmeg

1½ teaspoons ground cinnamon

½ teaspoon allspice

You can make this ahead of time, and you can snack on it (a little) because you won't be using the whole loaf for the pudding (you'll only use about three-quarters of the loaf).

Preheat the oven to 350°F. Line an 8 by 11-inch metal baking pan with parchment paper.

In a mixing bowl, combine the coconut oil, molasses, yogurt, apple-sauce, eggs, vanilla, and brown sugar. Blend together.

In a separate bowl, whisk together the flour, baking powder, baking soda, salt, ginger, cloves, nutmeg, cinnamon, and allspice. Then add the dry ingredients to the wet ingredients and blend well.

Pour the mixture into the baking pan and bake for 40 minutes, or until a knife inserted into the gingerbread comes out clean. Let cool. Store remaining gingerbread in an airtight container at room temperature for up to 3 days, or for a week in the fridge.

twin tip

Why do we mix dry ingredients separately? This ensures that some key baking ingredients are well blended before we add them to the wet ingredients. Otherwise, a crucial ingredient like baking soda or baking powder might not get dispersed enough to do its job.

pineapple upside-down carrot cake

MAKES 8 TO 10 SERVINGS   PREP TIME: 30 minutes   COOK TIME: 50 minutes

CAKE

1 cup canned crushed pineapple (very well drained)

1½ cups unbleached all-purpose flour

1 teaspoon baking powder

1 teaspoon baking soda

1 teaspoon ground cinnamon

½ teaspoon ground nutmeg

½ teaspoon allspice

½ teaspoon ground ginger

¼ teaspoon salt

½ cup unsalted butter, softened

2 eggs

1 cup granulated sugar

½ cup plain full-fat Greek yogurt

1 teaspoon vanilla extract

½ cup chopped pecans

2 cups peeled, shredded carrots (about 2½ carrots)

We make this cake for our parents' anniversary because it was the cake they had at their wedding (and our mom's favorite).

The base for this cake actually comes from a coffee cake recipe we make every Christmas—it's on our blog—but we add spices, carrots, and pineapple to this one. We appreciate a cake that has more going on than just flour.

Even though this cake is not as tall as a regular Bundt cake, we bake it in a Bundt pan because it creates sweet, buttery, caramelized sides and it looks pretty. We normally like icing on cakes, but this cake doesn't need it—it's perfect as is.

Preheat the oven to 350°F and thoroughly grease a Bundt pan (preferably nonstick) with butter.

To make the cake, start by draining the crushed pineapple by mashing it down with a spoon in a fine-mesh sieve so all of the liquid comes out (this is important).

In a medium bowl, whisk together the flour, baking powder, baking soda, cinnamon, nutmeg, allspice, ginger, and salt. Set aside.

Using a stand or hand mixer, mix the butter, eggs, granulated sugar, yogurt, and vanilla in a large bowl until they reach a creamy, even consistency. Stir in the flour mixture and blend.

Add the pecans, carrots, and drained crushed pineapple. (Scrape the sides and bottom of the bowl to make sure all the ingredients are blended.) Set aside.

→

TOPPING

2 tablespoons unsalted butter, melted

¼ cup packed light brown sugar

6 canned pineapple rings

twin tip

Brown sugar can get hard over time, and if it does, it's hard to work with and impossible to measure. If this happens to you, put the sugar in a closed container along with a piece of bread, and the sugar will magically soften in a few days. If you're in a hurry, you can place the sugar in a glass bowl, put a damp dish towel on top of the bowl, and microwave the sugar for 20 seconds at a time until it softens. (It won't take long.)

To make the topping, melt the butter in a small saucepan and pour around the base of the Bundt pan. Sprinkle the brown sugar on top of the butter, then place the pineapple rings on top. Pour the batter over the pineapple rings. The batter will not fill up the whole pan, but that is fine.

Bake for 50 to 55 minutes in the center of the oven. The cake is done when a knife inserted into it comes out clean.

Cool the cake for 15 minutes. Remove it from the Bundt pan by placing a plate on top of the pan and then flipping it over. Enjoy warm or chilled. Store in an airtight container at room temperature for up to 2 days or in the fridge for up to 4 days.

the ultimate peanut butter cookies

MAKES 24 COOKIES   PREP TIME: 20 minutes   COOK TIME: 20 to 24 minutes

¾ cup plus 2 tablespoons sugar

1 egg

1 cup unsweetened peanut butter (creamy or crunchy)

½ teaspoon baking soda

½ teaspoon baking powder

twin tips

Grease your teaspoon with cooking spray before you use it to scoop the dough. This will make the dough slide out easily.

If you buy the kind of peanut butter that has oil on top, be sure to stir it well before you take the peanut butter from the jar.

We've experimented a ton with peanut butter cookies. We've tried various amounts of sugar, eggs, baking soda, and baking powder. We've added and subtracted different types of flours. Now, we present the perfect PB cookie! It's just sweet enough, light in texture, and sublimely tasty.

Preheat the oven to 350°F and line a baking sheet with parchment paper.

In a medium bowl, beat together ¾ cup of the sugar and the egg, using either a hand or stand mixer, until the ingredients are creamed together evenly.

Add the peanut butter, baking soda, and baking powder and mix well.

Put the remaining 2 tablespoons of sugar in a small bowl.

Scoop out about 2 teaspoons of dough, form a ball, and roll the ball in the sugar. Place half of the balls on the baking sheet and, using a fork, gently press down on top of each cookie to make a crisscross pattern.

Bake for 10 minutes. Cool for 5 minutes, remove from the baking sheet, and then repeat with the second batch of cookies. Store in an airtight container for up to 2 days on the counter or up to a week in the fridge.

nutty oatmeal cookies

1 cup unsalted butter, softened

1 cup packed light brown sugar

¼ cup granulated sugar

2 eggs

2 teaspoons vanilla extract

1 cup unbleached all-purpose flour

1 cup old-fashioned rolled oats (not quick oats)

1 teaspoon baking soda

½ teaspoon salt

½ cup chopped pecans

1 cup unsweetened shredded coconut

1¼ cups dried cranberries (sweetened)

½ cup sliced almonds

twin tip

Cookie scoopers make life easy, and they're the best way to make sure your cookies are the right size and shape. We highly recommend them! You will end up using them to fill muffin tins, measure out pancake batter, and much more.

Some of our favorite ingredients—oats, coconut, almonds, pecans, and cranberries—come together in this recipe to create chewy cookie goodness. We count this dessert as healthy fuel before doing any physical activities—a little sugar boost never hurt anyone.

Preheat the oven to 350°F and line a baking sheet with parchment paper.

Using a stand or hand mixer, cream the butter, brown sugar, and granulated sugar together until they reach an even, creamy consistency. Add the eggs and vanilla and mix until evenly blended.

In a separate bowl, mix the flour, oats, baking soda, and salt. Add the dry ingredients to the wet mixture and mix until blended. Add the pecans, coconut, cranberries, and almonds and mix until blended.

Drop by tablespoons onto the baking sheet. Bake for 12 to 14 minutes or until golden brown. Remove and let cool for about 10 minutes before enjoying (if you can wait that long—we usually can't). Store in an airtight container at room temperature for 2 days or in the fridge for a week.

NOTE

If you don't want to bake the cookies all at once, put the dough on a piece of wax or parchment paper, shaping it into a log. Then roll the cookie-dough log up in the wax or parchment paper and store it in the freezer in a zip-top bag to cut and bake as you wish.

7
drinks & smoothies

If you're like us, you have a lot on your plate—whether it's school, sports, theater, music, chores, we could go on and on. That's why smoothies are awesome. You can blend them in just minutes, and drink them on the run.

Sometimes, on the other hand, it's nice to kick back and relax with a cool drink like a Watermelon Fresca (page 177), or cozy up with a Pumpkin Spice au Lait (page 171).

For days when you're under the weather, we also have a special recipe, Ginger "Aid" (page 178), from our mom, Cricket. We swear by it.

You can use any type of blender to make drinks and smoothies, but we happen to use a high-speed blender called a Vitamix that we bought with our own money. When we were young, we used to hang out in front of the Vitamix demo table at Whole Foods and wait for the samples. The demo person would invite us to press the buttons because we stood there so long waiting for the next recipe to sample. We begged our parents to buy a Vitamix (we were ten, and yes, we know that's a weird toy). They said no, but they said we could save up for it.

Two years later, we had enough money, and it's our number one household love (aside from our parents and pets). So, as you learn to cook, think about saving up for additions to your own kitchen tool kit.

berry blast smoothie

1 cup milk (see page 15)

⅓ cup plain Greek yogurt
(2% or full-fat)

1 ripe banana

⅓ cup blueberries
(fresh or frozen)

4 large strawberries
(fresh or frozen)

1 tablespoon shelled hemp seeds
(optional; see page 174)

Toppings (see below)

twin tip

Don't peel a banana when it's
green. It's not good yet, and
it will have a weird dry taste
and texture. Wait until it's totally
yellow or just starting to get
brown spots.

We keep berries and other fruits in our freezer year-round, so
they'll always be there when we need them—for instance, when
we want to make this simple smoothie, which is generally once
a week. Depending on how much time we have to eat this,
we either enjoy it in a glass or put it in a smoothie bowl and
decorate the top with fruits, nuts, or seeds.

Put the milk in a blender. Add the yogurt, banana, blueberries,
strawberries, and hemp seeds, and blend until smooth.

Fill a glass and slurp it up, or slow it down and turn it into a
smoothie bowl and add your favorite toppings.

TOPPING OPTIONS

Almond butter or peanut butter,
to dollop or drizzle (make it
drizzly by heating a dollop in the
microwave for 10 to 15 seconds)

Almonds

Bananas

Blackberries

Blueberries

Cacao nibs

Chia seeds

Dates

Granola

Mint leaves

Pecans

Pomegranate seeds

Puffed rice cereal

Raspberries

Shredded coconut

Strawberries

Sunflower seeds

Walnuts

pineapple banana smoothie

MAKES 1 SERVING   PREP TIME: 2 minutes

¾ cup milk (see page 15; we tend to use plain almond milk)

1 ripe banana (fresh or frozen)

1 cup fresh, chopped pineapple

Optional superchargers:
1 tablespoon shelled hemp seeds (see page 174) added while blending or 1 tablespoon chia seeds stirred in after blending

twin tip

Watch out for chia seeds getting stuck in your teeth. If this happens to someone else, quietly give the person a heads-up. Also, when your friends slurp down a smoothie, they'll likely have smile marks left that are the color of that smoothie. Nice to tell someone . . . or not, if it's entertaining.

This is a really refreshing drink. It's a go-to for us during sports season because it's rich in potassium from the bananas, and it's a favorite during the winter flu season because pineapple has a ton of vitamin C. So yeah . . . we enjoy this year-round!

Place the milk, banana, and pineapple in a blender. Add the hemp seeds, if using. Blend until all the ingredients are pureed smoothly. After blending, stir in the chia seeds, if using, and serve.

NOTE

Both hemp seeds and chia seeds have loads of nutrition. We add the chia seeds *after* blending because when we leave them whole, they hold water like little globules, boosting our hydration levels during sports.

perfect pumpkin spice au lait

MAKES 1 SERVING   PREP TIME: 5 minutes   COOK TIME: 5 minutes

1 cup milk (see page 15)

1 tablespoon coconut oil

1 tablespoon light brown sugar

1 tablespoon plus 1 teaspoon pumpkin puree (make sure this is plain pumpkin, not sweetened pumpkin or pumpkin pie puree)

¼ teaspoon pumpkin pie spice mix, store-bought or homemade (recipe follows)

Ground nutmeg for topping (optional)

We're wild about pumpkin, and when we started writing this cookbook, we went a little crazy with the pumpkin recipes. We've pared them down to our favorites, including this light, frothy pumpkin spice perfection in a mug.

This drink doesn't have any coffee in it like most *au lait* drinks you'll see in a café, but we call it an *au lait* because the base is "with milk," which is *au lait* in French.

Add the milk, coconut oil, brown sugar, pumpkin puree, and pumpkin pie spice to a medium saucepan. Cook over medium-high heat, whisking until the coconut oil has melted.

Enjoy as is or transfer to a blender and blend on high speed for 15 to 20 seconds, until the mixture is light and frothy. Pour into a mug and sprinkle some fresh nutmeg on top.

pumpkin pie spice mix

MAKES APPROXIMATELY ½ CUP   PREP TIME: 5 minutes

⅓ cup ground cinnamon

1 tablespoon ground ginger

1 tablespoon ground nutmeg

1½ teaspoons ground cloves

1½ teaspoons allspice

It's easy to make your own pumpkin pie spice mix. This recipe is based on one from the *Farmer's Almanac*. We like to keep pumpkin pie spice in a shaker so we can sprinkle it on hot cider, pancakes, French toast, caramelized bananas, yogurt, apples, and ice cream.

Put all the ingredients into a jar with a lid and shake well. Store in a dry area with other spices for up to 6 months.

green power smoothie

½ cup milk (see page 15)

½ cup water

1 cup loosely packed baby spinach

1 celery stalk, quartered

1 apple, any kind, cored and sliced

½ cup diced pineapple (see Note)

2–4 fresh mint leaves

twin tip

Always add liquids to your blender first, before adding other ingredients, because the blender blades have an easier time churning the solid ingredients when they are immersed in liquid.

The ingredients in this smoothie come together to create a sweet, refreshing, nutrition-packed drink with just a touch of mint.

We like the texture of baby spinach here. Sometimes the bigger, more wrinkly spinach tastes dry, and you don't want that dry spinach taste in your smoothie!

We use a ton of pineapple in our recipes because we always have more than one giant pineapple in our kitchen waiting to ripen, along with bowls of it cut up in our fridge. If you find it a pain to cut up a pineapple (see Notes), you can buy precut pineapple in the produce section or use the canned version.

Add the milk, water, spinach, celery, apple, pineapple, and 2 to 4 mint leaves (depending on how much you like mint) to a blender and blend until smooth. Add 2 ice cubes if you want your drink chilled.

NOTE

Cutting up a pineapple is easier than it looks, but ask your parents to help you if you're not yet skilled with big knives. Here's how to do it:

Cut off the top of the pineapple using a very sharp or serrated knife. (Keep the fingers on your free hand well away from the knife.)

Next, slice off the bottom of the pineapple so it can stand up straight. Then slice it in half lengthwise.

After that, slice down the sides to remove the skin, holding the pineapple at the top with your free hand so you don't cut your fingers. Cut each half into spears, cutting around the core. Discard the core and chop the spears into small bites.

peanut butter & banana smoothie

MAKES 1 SERVING   PREP TIME: 3 minutes

1 cup milk (see page 15)

3 tablespoons unsweetened peanut butter

1 ripe banana (fresh or frozen)

4 ice cubes (skip the ice if you're using a frozen banana)

1 tablespoon shelled hemp seeds (optional)

Sliced bananas, slivered almonds, coconut flakes, maple syrup, or chocolate chips/ shavings for topping smoothie bowl (optional)

We love the combination of peanut butter and bananas. This shake fills us up for a long time, so it's great for breakfast or for fueling up before or after a game, practice, hike, workout, or other sweaty activity!

If you aren't familiar with shelled hemp seeds, they're rich in protein and in healthy fats, so adding them to a smoothie is a great way to get an extra dose of nutrition. However, this shake tastes just as good without them.

Put the milk in a blender. Add the peanut butter, banana, ice cubes, and hemp seeds. Blend until smooth.

Enjoy in a glass, or pour into a smoothie bowl and add your favorite toppings.

VARIATION

Want to add chocolate? (Dumb question.) Add 1 tablespoon of unsweet-ened cocoa powder and blend.

soothing vanilla milk

1 cup milk (see page 15)

½ teaspoon vanilla extract

2 teaspoons light brown sugar

This is a sleepy-time drink we like to have as we're winding down before bed, especially during a stressful week. It's also a great way to enjoy milk if (like us) you aren't a big fan of plain milk.

This drink was an Adirondack staple of our mom and all her cousins when they were growing up. It's cold there at night in the summers, so they'd cozy up in front of the fire and sip it.

Put the milk, vanilla, and brown sugar in a saucepan and heat until warm, about 4 minutes. Don't let the mixture boil. Pour into a mug and get cozy.

watermelon fresca

MAKES 4 SERVINGS   PREP TIME: 10 minutes

4 cups 1-inch-cubed watermelon (unseeded)

2 cups club soda

Ice for serving

Mint leaves for garnish (optional)

The first time we did a *Rachael Ray* episode, they had a bottled watermelon drink in the dressing room. It was delicious, but in the stores, it's crazy expensive. So we made our own, and it's easy and truly tastes of summer. If you're like us, you'll also drink this during a snowstorm to have happy thoughts of summer ahead.

By the way, *fresca* means "fresh" in Spanish . . . and this is very *fresca*!

Put the watermelon in a blender and blend until smooth. Pour the puree through a sieve into a pitcher. Add the club soda.

To enjoy, add some ice to a glass, pour this lovely watermelon fresca over the ice, and add a mint leaf for color and its beautiful aroma. And *ya está*—fancy fresca!

NOTE

We keep the watermelon fresca in our SodaStream containers, but you can also store it in club soda bottles. Just don't add ice to the bottles, because it will dilute the sweetness.

ginger "aid"

MAKES 1 SERVING   PREP TIME: 10 minutes

1 cup boiling hot water

1 tablespoon peeled, freshly grated ginger (see Twin Tips, page 115)

Juice from ½ lemon (about 1 tablespoon)

1 tablespoon honey

1 teaspoon raw unfiltered apple cider vinegar (we use Dr. Bragg's brand)

Pinch of cayenne pepper

This is a drink our mom makes for us when we have a cold, a stomach bug, or a fever. It's a cure-all that clears out a stuffy chest and sinuses immediately and settles our stomachs as well.

We've tried to get our grandmothers to drink this when they aren't feeling well. One likes it, the other not so much. This drink has a lot of zing to it, so be prepared!

Pour the boiling water into a mug with the ginger. Let steep for 2 minutes, then pour the ginger water through a sieve (fine strainer) into your favorite mug to separate the ginger out. Add the lemon juice, honey, apple cider vinegar, and just a light sprinkling (like a flick of your hand) of the cayenne pepper. Enjoy and get well soon.

acknowledgments

To our parents, for encouraging and inspiring us—we will forever be thankful.

To our grandparents, aunts, uncles, cousins, and friends—Ali, Annie, Phoebe, Franny, Quinn, Eshaa, Ellrose, Kate, Joseph, Megan, Parker, Jack, Sara, Lucy, Jaelyn, Nina, Miles, Jojo, Liam, and Abby—we're incredibly grateful for your support and your belief in us.

A huge thank-you to Rachael Ray for being such a kind and generous mentor—and to Chelsea Meyer, a producer on *Rachael Ray*.

Heartfelt thanks also to an awesome group of chefs and other professionals who have helped us in so many ways—whether it was providing us with amazing opportunities, cheering us on, or sharing their expertise with us. We are grateful in particular to Chloe Coscarelli, Marcus Samuelsson, Maria Loi, Bill Telepan, Bryce Shuman, Cesar Gutierrez, Tico, Nancy Eastman and Wellness in the Schools, the Michael Graves Group, Lillipies, Jammin' Crêpes, WildFlour Bakery, Pennington Market, Mr. Cimorelli, TVS, iTi Tropical, and the Food Network.

A big thank-you as well to so many people in our wonderful community for supporting us in ways too numerous to count. Special thanks to our teachers, advisors, coaches, and family friends: Pam McLean, Kelly Ford Buckley, Mr. and Mrs. Grausman, Carol Manikin, Mrs. Flory, Mrs. Cutler, "milo," the Terrys, the Clarks, the Diggans, the Pelosos, the Gallaghers, the Causing/Waanderses, the Dixons, the Vaugheys, the Staikoses, the Doshis, the Suraces, the Dahls, the Dorans, the Waxmans, the Bennetts, the Thompsons, the Asplundh/Gardners, and the Hanlons.

We are also grateful to our agent, Margot Maley Hutchison, for her enthusiasm for this project; to our editor, Kelly Snowden, for giving us the opportunity to share our recipes; to our photographer, Justin Walker, for his wonderful photos; and to the entire production team at Ten Speed Press.

We also thank each of you who took time to give us likes on our foodie posts!

dedication

Dedicated to our parents, for their unconditional love.

index